THE BIBLE IN 52 WEEKS FOR KIDS

THE BIBLE IN 52 WEEKS FOR KIDS

AN EASY BIBLE STUDY

BONNIE RICKNER JENSEN

callisto publishing
an imprint of Sourcebooks

Illustrations by Agnieszka Żylińska-Rękas
Series Designer: Liz Cosgrove
Art Director: Lisa Schreiber
Art Producer: Stacey Stambaugh
Editor: Pamela Bobowicz
Production Editor: Rachel Taenzler
Production Designer: Jeffrey Piekarz

Published by Callisto Publishing LLC C/O Sourcebooks LLC
P.O. Box 4410, Naperville, Illinois 60567-4410
(630) 961-3900
callistopublishing.com

Library of Congress Cataloging-in-Publication Data is on file with the publisher.

This product conforms to all applicable CPSC and CPSIA standards.

Source of Production: Wing King Tong Paper Products Co. Ltd. Shenzhen, Guangdong Province, China
Date of Production: January 2026
Run Number: 5050277

Printed and bound in China.
WKT 10 9 8 7 6 5 4 3 2 1

To my parents,
Alvin and
Barbara, who
showed me the
love of God
through the
love they gave.

—**BRJ**

CONTENTS

INTRODUCTION

WHEN I WAS A CHILD, I sang in church with my family. I was nervous, but the words of the songs made me feel brave. I was surrounded by my family and friends, singing about God's perfect love in front of my entire church community. My dad played guitar, and my mom played accordion. I sang loud and out of tune. We sang songs like "What a Friend We Have in Jesus." As I grew, I learned how real and important His friendship is.

Imagine having a friend who wants only good things for you. A friend who *never* says a bad word about you. A friend you can talk to in the middle of the night or when you're having a really difficult day or any time at all. Jesus is that friend. He knows what you've been through, what you're going through, and what's coming for you ahead. He sees you in everything you do, and His love for you won't stop no matter what you do.

That's one of the beautiful things about reading the Bible—you get to learn about love, obedience, sacrifice, forgiveness, faith, hope, and so much more.

The Bible is a book about God's perfect love. It tells of His plan to give us the gift of **eternal** life. The hero in God's story is Jesus, His only Son. Jesus carried out God's plan to save us.

God has a plan for you, too. Your life is special to Him, and He has big plans and a purpose for you. Through reading the Bible, you'll get to know God and understand His ways. There's no greater love in the universe than God's love. You'll see that in many of the stories in the Bible. God asks certain things of us, His people, and He stays with us as we complete them. We might make a mistake once in a while, but God never leaves us. He's a forgiving, compassionate Father who loves us as we are. There's no greater proof of His love than what Jesus did. And *you're* the reason He did it.

Reading the Bible will make your spirit strong the way exercising makes your body strong. A healthy spirit keeps your heart brave. You'll meet many different people and can learn from each of their examples. A good thing to do while reading is find a friend or grown-up to discuss your readings with. You can ask questions, discuss how the readings make you feel, and share the incredible experience of getting to know God with someone you love. Because the best part about reading God's Word? Discovering God's love for you.

I'm praying you grow stronger in His love every day.

Bonnie

HOW TO USE THIS BOOK

THE GOAL OF THIS BOOK is to introduce you to all 66 books of the Bible in one year. It's designed to get you excited about reading it on your own. You might be thinking, *Sixty-six books in one year?!* Don't worry—there are 52 weeks in one year, so you'll be introduced to one or two books each week through characters, quotes, and brief readings.

The Bible is unlike any other book in the world. It's written by *many* people who were **inspired** by one almighty God. The coolest part? God knew you'd be reading it! He's excited for you to find out how much He loves you.

The Bible is thousands of years old, but the wisdom in it gives us a new heart filled with hope, courage, and love. It teaches us the best way to live, by following the One who loves us the most. The Apostle Paul said, "Do not conform to the pattern of this world, but be transformed by the renewing of your mind. Then you will be able to test and approve what God's will is—His good, pleasing and perfect will" (Romans 12:2). The will of God is simply the way of God.

Reading through the Bible is a big goal. This book makes it easy for you to step into it slowly, one day at a time. Reading the Bible every day is a good habit. I hope this book will encourage you to do that. As you read and think about the people, verses, and chapters, you'll get to know God and you'll get to know yourself. Developing your own relationship with God is inspiring and uplifting. He has a perfect plan for your life, and as you read the Bible and get to know His way, you'll see your life's plan stretching out before you, waiting for you to be ready. He wants everyone to spend **eternity** in the presence of His perfect love. God's plan to make that happen is the most valuable gift the Bible holds.

You will encounter some challenging topics as you read. The Bible covers many years, perspectives, and people. If you read something in the Bible that you don't understand, or something that feels too mature or too difficult to think about on your own, reach out to your parent, teacher, religious leader, or a friend and ask them to read that chapter with you.

Pick up this book any time of the day you choose. Read an entry for one day. Open your Bible and dig deeper to discover more. Ask God to make your heart and mind eager to learn. You're going to like getting close to your Creator. He thinks you're *amazing*!

WHAT MATERIALS DO I NEED?

- **This book.**
- **The Bible.** The verses you'll see in this book are from the New International Version. You can use any version or translation you'd like! You may also benefit from an electronic or audio version that can be downloaded.
- **Notebook, journal, or tablet.** This will be helpful if you want to take extra notes or keep track of passages that you want to read again when you need guidance.
- **Pen, pencil, colored pencils, markers, crayons.**

WHAT'S IN THIS BOOK?

THIS BOOK GIVES YOU A GLIMPSE into all 66 books in the Bible, in order from Genesis to Revelation. There are 52 one-week sections, so you'll be traveling through the entire Bible in one year. Each day of the week includes something to help you understand the book or books of the week. It could be verses and chapters to read, introductions to some of the famous people in the Bible, or a quote to reflect on. Each daily entry is followed by a short explanation to expand its meaning and help you better understand God's message. After you read a daily entry, take a few minutes to think about how God's Word applies to your life and the things you go through.

You'll find plenty of room for your thoughts, questions, and prayers throughout this book. There are guided questions for discussion and reflection. Some will encourage you to gather friends, family, or community members to work together and share God's love. You can use these questions and activities to grow your relationship with God.

As you do the good work of being kind, forgiving others, and sharing God's love, I hope you learn to love the special person He created in *you*. You're irreplaceable!

GREAT ON YOUR OWN OR WITH A FRIEND

You can dive into this book on your own. You can go through it with your parents, siblings, or friends. The important thing is to ask God to prepare your heart to learn.

MY LIFE WITH GOD

God knows you best. His Word teaches you to see yourself the way He created you: marvelous and wonderful! The more we learn about God's infinite love for us, the braver we become to live a more confident, kind, and loving life.

YOU CAN DO IT!

This book will encourage you to see yourself as God sees you in His perfect love. It will build your trust in God. If you miss a daily reading, it's easy to catch up. Don't feel defeated! You can open His Word at any time and find something to lift you up like a balloon.

WEEK #1

God Sees Great Things in You

DAILY READINGS & REFLECTIONS

Day 1: Read Genesis 1–3.
God created everything that exists—every plant and animal, the stars, and even you! It all reflects the **miracle** of His love.

Day 2: "When God created mankind, He made them in the likeness of God." (from Genesis 5:1)
God wants us to be like Him. Our actions should always reflect the love of God and make the world a brighter place.

Day 3: Meet Noah (from Genesis 6:9–22).
God decided to destroy all living things with a flood. But Noah was a good man and his faith in God made him part of God's brand-new start for our world.

Day 4: Read Genesis 17:1–22.
God appeared to Abram, now known as Abraham, and told him he would be "the father of many nations." Abraham was 99 years old and didn't have any children of his own. But God's plans for our lives happens in His time.

Day 5: "On the mountain of the Lord it will be provided." (from Genesis 22:14)
God tested Abraham in a *big* way, and when Abraham obeyed, God blessed him. God may test us, but He will *always* provide a way through.

Day 6: Meet Joseph (from Genesis 37, 39–45).
Joseph was his father's most beloved son, which made his brothers jealous. The brothers planned to get rid of him, but God had special plans for Joseph's life.

Day 7: Read Genesis 50:15–21.
God asks us to forgive those who have wronged or hurt us. Even when we are still hurting, forgiveness helps to heal our heart. It is God's love in action.

Genesis is the very first book of the Bible, and what a way to begin your journey! Genesis helps us understand God's vision for the world—and our unique role in it. It's about creation and obedience, which means to follow God's way.

God created every part of our big, beautiful world. As the population on earth grew, God saw that the people had lost their way—they forgot about Him. Sparing only Noah, his family, and two of every living creature on earth, God flooded His creation and began again.

God shows us over and over again how the faith and obedience of His people are tested. Faith is trusting God completely. Being tested is a hard challenge to face. You might feel tested when you choose to do what's right, even when your friends or peers suggest a different way. God allows these tests to challenge us in order to build our faith and make our relationship with Him stronger.

The unique set of traits God gave you is His way of setting you apart to follow His plan for your life. Yes—God has a specific plan for *you*! He will reveal it to you in perfect timing throughout your life.

God's plan for Noah was to build an ark. God's plan for Abraham was to become the father of many nations. God's plan for Joseph was to become a king and help people. The greatest thing God sees in you is your faith in Him. He's preparing you for your unique and beautiful life.

BIG QUESTIONS

1. Every day is a chance to look in the mirror and thank God for creating the awesome and only YOU. What do you love most about the way God made you?

2. Love is a superpower that helps us do what's right even when it's hard. Can you think of a time it was hard to follow God's way and do the right thing? How did your love for God—or for another person—help you decide what to do?

3. We make *many* choices every day. How can you ask God to help you make kind and loving decisions for your life?

WORDS AND WISDOM TO SHARE

God created each of us with special gifts. Sit down with your family or a few friends and say something you like about each person. Write down the special traits and qualities that others said about you so you can read them when you need to feel God's love.

GOD AND ME

Everything you see is a part of God's great, big, beautiful world. Draw a picture of something in God's creation that reflects *His* greatness and inspires you.

WEEK #2
God Is for You!

DAILY READINGS & REFLECTIONS

Day 1: Meet Moses (from Exodus 2–3).
When Moses didn't think he was good enough to lead his people out of suffering, God told him, "Don't worry. I'll go with you." God won't let you face anything alone.

Day 2: Meet Aaron (from Exodus 4).
Moses was unsure about speaking to Pharaoh on his own, so God sent his brother Aaron with him. God brings the right people to help us when we need them.

Day 3: Read Exodus 14.
When God's people were about to be overcome, God parted the Red Sea to save them. Even when you feel afraid, you can be brave, because nothing is too big for God.

Day 4: Read Exodus 16.
God's people grumbled to Moses, despite the miracles they witnessed. God's love for us is unstoppable, no matter what. Gratitude brings us closer to Him.

Day 5: Read Exodus 20:1–17.
God gives us the Ten Commandments to live by to keep our lives on the right path. God's commandments are for our good because His love for us is perfect.

Day 6: "I will do the very thing you have asked, because I am pleased with you and I know you by name." (from Exodus 33:17)
God said these words to Moses, and He would say them to you, too. He knows *you*. He knows your name. God recognizes your voice. God is for you.

Day 7: "The Israelites had done all the work just as the Lord commanded Moses." (from Exodus 39:42)
God gave His people every skill they needed to do the work He asked them to do. God will use your talent for a special purpose, too.

The book of Exodus reveals God's compassion, power, and patience. God saw His people suffering in Egypt and His heart was moved. He heard their cries and saved them.

God displayed His power through Moses, a great prophet and a humble leader. Moses was chosen to do a huge task. At first, Moses didn't think God made the right choice in him. Standing up to Pharaoh meant Moses had to do something almost impossible. But Moses learned, just like we do, that God doesn't make wrong choices!

If God is for us, *anything* is possible. What does it mean to have God on your side? God is *for* you when you use your gifts. God is *for* you when you serve others. God is *for* you when you love people and show kindness.

God proved over and over again that He was with Moses. Moses felt just like we do sometimes—nervous about doing something we're not very good at. But courage is one of God's specialties. If we ask Him for it, we can trust He'll give it to us. Being brave can teach us how strong we are—and make us even stronger.

BIG QUESTIONS

1. How do you ask God for courage when you need to be brave?

2. How do you feel after you've made it through something you were nervous about?

3. God has commandments for how He wants us to treat others. Do you have rules for how you want to be treated?

WORDS AND WISDOM TO SHARE

God is for you, even when you're afraid or don't think you have what it takes. When we encourage others, we get stronger, too. Write a little note to someone in your life to help them feel brave. Let them know God is for them and that you believe in them.

GOD AND ME

Make a list of the times you trusted God to help you overcome your fear or get through a difficult time.

WEEK #3

Blessed by Being Close to God

DAILY READINGS & REFLECTIONS

Day 1: Read Leviticus 9.
Moses called on Aaron and his sons to make offerings for God. Once they'd made these offerings, they were blessed. Following God makes us a blessing to the people around us.

Day 2: "Each of you must respect your mother and father." (from Leviticus 19:3)
God asks us to respect our parents. It is one of the ways we honor Him.

Day 3: Read Leviticus 19:1–19.
God set many rules for His people to follow. Love is most important to God. Treating others with love and respect is an important way to show we put God first in our lives.

Day 4: "You are to be holy to Me because I, the Lord, am holy, and I have set you apart from the nations to be My own." (from Leviticus 20:26)
There's no better way for us to feel like we belong than to be called *God's own*.

Day 5: Meet the High Priest (from Leviticus 21:10).
High priests were important figures. They were set apart and **holy**. They taught God's laws, made sure the laws were followed, and prayed for God's people.

Day 6: Read Leviticus 22:31.
When we follow God, we should never use His name in a disrespectful way. Honoring God with our words and the way we talk is a good way to become closer to Him.

Day 7: "When you reap the harvest of your land, do not reap to the very edges of your field or gather the gleanings of your harvest. Leave them for the poor and for the foreigner residing among you." (from Leviticus 23:22)
God wants us to have compassion for those in need.

The book of Leviticus reveals how important it is to God that we have a relationship with Him. He wants to be close to us. God is holy, which means He is completely pure. In this book, God is very specific about how His people needed to offer sacrifices for their sins. For God to be able to dwell among them, their sins had to be atoned for, which means the people had to make amends.

Today, this helps us understand why God sent His Son, Jesus Christ, to be the perfect and final sacrifice for the sins of the world. By accepting what Jesus did for us, there is *nothing* keeping us from being close to God. We are made holy like God through the perfect sacrifice of Jesus.

Our actions should always reflect God's love. It's the best way to bring His goodness and holiness into this world. When others see your kindness, or when they see you setting a good example, they'll be inspired to do the same. That's how God works through you to bring His perfect love to those around you.

BIG QUESTIONS

1. Serving a holy God makes us lighthouses of love. Have you shined God's love on someone this week? How?

2. In God's eyes, everyone we meet is like a neighbor, especially those in need. Can you think of a way you might help someone this week?

3. Have you ever chosen to be different from others? Maybe they wanted you to do something you didn't want to do? How did you choose to follow God's way instead?

WORDS AND WISDOM TO SHARE

Start a conversation with your family or a friend and talk about how you each honor God and why. Write down some of the responses so you can look back if you need inspiration in the future.

GOD AND ME

Write down the names of some people you know who dared to be different by obeying God. What did they do that you can do in your life—now or in the future?

WEEK #4

Putting Others First

DAILY READINGS & REFLECTIONS

Day 1: "The Lord bless you and keep you; the Lord make His face shine on you and be gracious to you; the Lord turn His face toward you and give you peace." (from Numbers 6:24–26)
God blessed His people and this verse is a blessing for you, too.

Day 2: Read Numbers 12:1–12.
Moses kept faith in God, prayed for the well-being of others, and didn't act proud. When we consider others and not just ourselves, we are humble in the same way.

Day 3: Read Numbers 13:17–30.
Caleb trusted God would keep His promise to His people. Remember that things won't always be easy, but we can trust God to be with us.

Day 4: "The Lord is slow to anger, abounding in love." (from Numbers 14:18)
God's way is one of **mercy**. We all get frustrated. We say things we don't mean. When we ask God to help us, we're reminded to act from love.

Day 5: Read Numbers 20:1–13.
God told Moses to pour water from a rock using his words, but Moses chose to do it differently. God's way is always best.

Day 6: Meet Balaam (from Numbers 22:1–38).
Balaam was asked to curse God's people. He refused, and God used him to bless His people instead. We should not do anything great or small to go against God.

Day 7: Meet Joshua (from Numbers 27:15–23).
God chose Joshua to lead the Israelites into the Promised Land. Joshua was humble and a good leader. When we use our gifts for the good of others, we serve God.

One of the things the book of Numbers teaches is how precious humility is. God values humility, which means being thankful to God for the blessings in our lives, and putting others first.

God's people were *continually* rebellious. Through their story, we learn that God's love and compassion are *constant* when we turn to Him with a humble heart.

God wouldn't have chosen Moses to be a leader if he didn't have a good heart. Moses cared about the people he was leading. Putting others first changes us in good ways. We learn that caring for other people brings joy. We learn that being a more loving person means we have more love for ourselves, too. Think about how powerful your life becomes when you put others first. When your mom is tired from working late, you might offer to help her clean instead of playing a game. When you're with a friend, maybe you let them choose what you'll do together. If you notice a neighbor working in their yard, you can put aside what you're doing to help them. Your actions impact everyone around you and bring your heart closer to God.

Being humble keeps God in the highest place and reminds us that no matter where we are, we're loved and valued exactly the same.

BIG QUESTIONS

1. Can you list a few ways you put others first this week? How did that make you feel?

2. Moses was raised in a royal household, but he understood that *everyone* God creates is valuable. What's a good way to help a friend know how special they are?

3. How would you explain what it means to be humble?

WORDS AND WISDOM TO SHARE

Make a list of three people who you will put first this week. This could be a friend, a parent, a sibling, a teacher, or neighbor. Beside each name, write down how you will help them. At the end of the week, look back at all you've done to share God's love.

GOD AND ME

Think about a recent situation where you might have acted in a more humble way. What could you have done differently? What will you do next time? Write down a simple prayer for practicing humility, so you'll always remember how important it is.

WEEK #5

Devoting Our Hearts to God

DAILY READINGS & REFLECTIONS

Day 1: Meet the Israelites (from Deuteronomy 1:3–11).
The Israelites are the descendants of Abraham, and *God's chosen people*. God made an everlasting **covenant** with Abraham.

Day 2: "The Lord your God has blessed you... He has watched over your journey...you have not lacked anything." (from Deuteronomy 2:7)
It's not easy to be patient when we're hoping for something. But God knows the right time for us.

Day 3: "Love the Lord your God with all your heart and with all your soul and with all your strength." (from Deuteronomy 6:5)
It's hard to hide our excitement when we're enthusiastic about something! Our love for God should be like that, too.

Day 4: Read Deuteronomy 28:1–14.
God gave His people laws to follow, and if they obeyed, His blessings would follow them all their life.

Day 5: Meet the Patriarchs (from Deuteronomy 29–30).
Abraham, Isaac, and Jacob are known as the patriarchs, which means the founders of the faith. God's covenant with Abraham continued through the following generations.

Day 6: "Let the beloved of the Lord rest secure in Him, for He shields him all day long." (Deuteronomy 33:12)
Picture yourself resting in a cozy hammock, safe and protected. That's what being secure in God is like.

Day 7: Read Deuteronomy 34.
Moses lived a long life, devoted to God. Trust God, and He will bless others through your words and actions.

In the book of Deuteronomy, Moses speaks to the Israelites about God's faithfulness and shares laws about how to live. Most importantly, Moses encourages them to stay devoted to God. Their journey to the Promised Land holds many lessons for us in devotion, discipline, patience, and love. God is with us throughout our lives as a loving Father who wants every good thing for us.

Deuteronomy shows how loyalty to God brings good things. We have chances to show our devotion to God by giving to the poor, helping our neighbor, and being a good friend.

Our pets are simple and honest examples of devotion. They adore us wholeheartedly. They want to obey us and they love spending time together. Our devotion to God should look a lot like that—our hearts adore Him, we want to obey Him, and we love spending time with Him. Time with God can be prayer, reading your Bible, or even taking a walk in nature to feel thankful for what He created.

BIG QUESTIONS

1. It's hard to feel loyal to someone when we've been hurt. How do you forgive a friend when they've hurt your feelings?

2. What does loyalty mean to you? Does your definition align with God's vision?

GOD AND ME

What does being devoted to God mean to you? Write a letter to God telling Him about your devotion, and how you'll stay committed to this as you grow.

WEEK #6

The Rewards of Following God

DAILY READINGS & REFLECTIONS

Day 1: Read Joshua 1:1–15.
God cheered on Joshua as he became the new leader of the Israelites. God is rooting for us in the same way today. *Be strong! Be courageous! I will* never *leave your side.*

Day 2: Meet Rahab (Joshua 2:2–22).
Rahab risked her life to protect the spies Joshua sent. Her actions saved her whole family. Helping others is a brave thing to do.

Day 3: Read Joshua 3:11–17.
God parted the waters of the Jordan River so His people could cross into the promised land. Miracles in the Bible are recorded to give us hope. With God, anything is possible!

Day 4: Read Joshua 6:1–20.
The walls around Jericho seemed impossible to get past! Joshua saw the walls crumble by obeying God. Trust God—He already knows our way through.

Day 5: Meet Caleb (from Joshua 14:6–15).
Caleb had the courage to trust God. In time, his faith was rewarded. God rewards us at the perfect time, when our heart is ready.

Day 6: "You know with all your heart and soul that not one of all the good promises the Lord your God gave you has failed. Every promise has been fulfilled." (from Joshua 23:14)
Take time to thank God every day.

Day 7: "Choose for yourselves this day whom you will serve." (from Joshua 24:15)
Obeying God is our choice. It's not always the easy path, but it leads us closer to God.

The book of Joshua highlights how obedience and trust led God's people to the reward of a blessed and beautiful land to call home. Learning to obey God's way will always bring rewards. Many of them will be simple, like helping others and showing gratitude. But each of those rewards fills our heart in ways nothing else can. That's how God's love works!

Rules are all around us. There are rules to follow at home and at school. There are laws we have to obey to make our towns and cities safe and orderly. When rules are broken, there are consequences. Just as we are disciplined for breaking rules, God would not be a loving Father if He didn't discipline us for our disobedience to Him. God loves and understands us. He knows we learn valuable lessons from the things we do wrong, and He teaches us through love and forgiveness. God knows that when we grow closer to Him, our desire to disobey fizzles out—and we begin to look forward to the rewards of following Him.

BIG QUESTIONS

1. God's biggest ask of us is learning to love others well. What are some little things you do to practice love and kindness toward others?

2. When we obey God, it makes us feel happier, too. Describe how you feel when you follow God's way. Compare that to how you feel when you *don't* follow God's way.

GOD AND ME

What does obedience mean to you? It can seem like a big word with a lot of demands. Put simply, the greatest commandments are these: Love God. Love others. Make a list of two things you can do every day to show your love for God and for others.

1.

2.

WEEK #7

Taking Care of Others

DAILY READINGS & REFLECTIONS

Day 1: Read Judges 2:1–10.
After Joshua died, the new generation forgot about God and turned away from Him. It can be easy to forget the good things people have done for us, but God wants you to keep those people in your heart.

Day 2: "Whenever the Lord raised up a judge for them, He was with the judge and saved them out of the hands of their enemies." (from Judges 2:18)
A judge was considered a hero, and God raised them up as an example for the people.

Day 3: Meet Othniel (from Judges 3:7–11).
Caleb's brother Othniel was a judge of Israel and a brave warrior for God's people.

Day 4: Meet Deborah (from Judges 4:1–14).
Deborah was a prophet, judge, and military leader. She led God's people for 60 years by helping them see that God was with them.

Day 5: "May all who love you be like the sun when it rises in its strength." (from Judges 5:31)
This is from the Song of Deborah. Loving God makes us shine like the sun! Kindness is the big, bright glow that warms a cold world.

Day 6: Meet Gideon (from Judges 6:11–18).
The angel of the Lord came to visit Gideon, and called him a mighty warrior. He asked the angel to give him a sign that God was with him. God is always there to give us courage.

Day 7: Read Judges 13.
Before he was born, an angel gave Samson's parents many rules to follow in order to have a son. They obeyed, and God blessed them.

The book of Judges gives us a true view of God's unstoppable compassion. He felt sympathetic toward the Israelites every time they disobeyed Him and ended up in terrible situations. God raises up people to be a blessing and take care of others. It's exciting to know that when we follow God, He gives us the courage, strength, and compassion to do great things.

Compassion is contagious. When we care about one another and the world God created, our light shines brighter—and that draws attention! When we live a life that looks like the goodness of God, others want to be like that, too. Sometimes people have to *see* the good to *be* the good. You know what else happens when we care for others? It makes our hearts feel closer to God, and that fills us with joy. Happy hearts are hard to hide!

Every day, God gives us a chance to be a caring, loving force in the world. From cheering up a friend who's having a bad day, to helping your parent make a meal for a sick neighbor, to filling the bird feeder in the backyard, *every* act of care matters.

BIG QUESTIONS

1. Do you remember a time when God's compassion and care for *you* was clear? Who did He send to help you?

2. Is there an act of care you've done this week? What was it? How did it make you feel?

3. What part of God's world do you feel a need to care for? It could be helping a neighbor, taking action to protect the environment, or something that calls you to use your unique gifts.

WORDS OF WISDOM TO SHARE

Create a circle of compassion with your family. Go around the circle and have each person share a story of someone going through a hard time. Pray for them. Then make a plan of action for how you can bring them comfort and compassion.

GOD AND ME

We all go through hard times. Write about a time when things were difficult, and how you felt God's comfort.

WEEK #8

A Loyal Heart

DAILY READINGS & REFLECTIONS

Day 1: Meet Naomi (from Ruth 1:1–5).
Naomi suffered a great loss, but God brought her comfort through the loyalty of her daughter-in-law, Ruth. God comforts us through people who love us.

Day 2: Meet Ruth (from Ruth 1:6–17).
Ruth refused to leave her mother-in-law, Naomi, after all that she'd been through. A good friend is a gift from God.

Day 3: Meet Boaz (from Ruth 2:1–11).
Boaz heard about Ruth's loyalty to Naomi, and became a big part of God's blessings for her. Your devotion to God and the people you love shines like the stars in the sky.

Day 4: Read Ruth 2:12–23.
Ruth's loyalty to Naomi led her straight to the blessings of God. We should take every chance we are given to be a loyal friend.

Day 5: "All the people of my town know that you are a woman of noble character." (from Ruth 3:11)
People respected Ruth for her loyalty to Naomi. The things we do show who we truly are.

Day 6: Read Ruth 4:1–14.
Boaz saw the goodness in Ruth and provided for her and Naomi in their time of need. Taking care of others is part of God's perfect care.

Day 7: "He will renew your life and sustain you in your old age." (from Ruth 4:15)
God constantly fills our life with new things to be thankful for. Every day, we have reasons, both big and small, to thank God.

The book of Ruth is about loyalty. Learning to be someone that others can count on is an admirable trait. Ruth proved her loyalty to Naomi by staying with her after she suffered the great loss of her husband and her sons. God provided for them and blessed both of their lives. Staying loyal to God brings good things to pass.

Being loyal means we can be trusted. If we hear something said about a friend when they're not around, we should stand up for them. Loyalty challenges us to tell the truth when it's not easy and to keep the promises we make. When we are committed to following God, we stay loyal to the way He asks us to live. Loving others is the best way to show how strong our loyalty to God is, because love is His greatest commandment.

BIG QUESTIONS

1. God knows that loyal friends are a blessing to us. Do you have a friend who is kind and loyal? What have you learned from them about loyalty?

2. How do you show that you're a loyal friend?

3. Has your loyalty to God ever been challenged in any way? What did you do?

WORDS AND WISDOM TO SHARE

Work with a family member or a friend to draw or write down some of the new, good things God has put in your life recently. How did you thank God for each one?

WEEK #9

A Humble Heart Plays a Big Part

DAILY READINGS & REFLECTIONS

Day 1: "Hannah was praying in her heart, and her lips were moving but her voice was not heard." (from 1 Samuel 1:13)
Hannah didn't need to use her voice to pray. God saw what was in her heart.

Day 2: Meet Samuel (from 1 Samuel 3).
Samuel worked in service to the Lord from when he was young. It honors God when we imitate Him.

Day 3: "Samuel served as leader of Israel, and told them, 'I will intercede with the Lord for you.'" (from 1 Samuel 7:5)
When Samuel says he'll intercede for the Israelites, it means he'll talk to God on their behalf. Praying for other people is a silent superpower. We can use it anytime, anywhere to help others.

Day 4: Read 1 Samuel 9:2–27.
God chose Saul from the smallest tribe in Israel to be a leader. More than once, God chose leaders who didn't feel qualified. But God knows us, and *He* believes in you.

Day 5: "People look at the outward appearance, but the Lord looks at the heart." (from 1 Samuel 16:7)
It's easy to only see what's outside, but remember to look within yourself and others.

Day 6: Meet David (from 1 Samuel 17).
David was the youngest of eight brothers. To those looking on, he was least likely to slay a giant. Remember, when you feel small, God sees you very differently.

Day 7: Read 1 Samuel 20:12–23.
Jonathan and David had a friendship bound by God's love. They promised to protect each other. Being a good friend reflects the character of God.

The book of 1 Samuel is an important reminder of how God sees us. God knows our thoughts and sees our heart—then nudges us toward the right path. If you ask your parents for permission to do something they know you're not ready for, their loving answer will be "not yet." Because God knows us, He responds the same way. When we pray for something we want or hope for, we often have to wait. But waiting is part of God's answer.

When David slayed Goliath, he knew it wasn't by his skill, size, strategy, or strength. His humble heart is the reason he was chosen. A humble heart keeps us from being selfish. A humble heart doesn't allow us to think we're more important than someone else. A humble heart is kind, quick to forgive, and good at putting God first. Sometimes God is the only one who can see how strong we are or how brave we can be.

BIG QUESTIONS

1. Sometimes we act out of pride instead of humility. Can you think of a time you acted out of pride? How did that make you feel? How did others respond to you?

2. What are you waiting for from God?

WORDS AND WISDOM TO SHARE

Ask a friend or family member to tell you their David vs. Goliath moment—when they overcame something that seemed impossible through their faith in God.

WEEK #10

God's Way Every Day

DAILY READINGS & REFLECTIONS

Day 1: Read 2 Samuel 5:1–5.
David was a teenager when he slayed Goliath, and 30 years old when he became king. God's plan and timing for us is perfect—don't ever doubt.

Day 2: "You, Sovereign Lord, have spoken, and with Your blessing the house of Your servant will be blessed forever." (from 2 Samuel 7:29)
This is a never-ending promise for those who serve God.

Day 3: Meet Mephibosheth (from 2 Samuel 9).
Jonathan's son, Mephibosheth, couldn't walk, so David promised to take care of him. Jonathan had been David's best friend. His loyalty to his friend blessed both families.

Day 4: "Then David said to Nathan, 'I have sinned against the Lord.'" (from 2 Samuel 12:13)
Nathan was a prophet in King David's court. God used him to confront David for his sin. God will bring people into our lives who help us be honest with ourselves.

Day 5: Meet Absalom (from 2 Samuel 14:25–33, 15:1–12).
Absalom was a handsome, charming, and dearly loved son of King David, but pride was his downfall.

Day 6: "You save the humble, but Your eyes are on the haughty to bring them low." (from 2 Samuel 22:28)
Haughty means arrogant or boastful. A haughty heart says, "Look at me!" A humble heart says, "Listen to God!"

Day 7: Read 2 Samuel 22:31–37.
King David wrote this song, which says, "As for God, His way is perfect." Staying close to God helps us follow His way.

The second book of Samuel shows us how dangerous it can be to go against God. We meet Absalom, a man who became too proud. He felt superior because of his good looks and his winning personality. Eventually, he did what he wanted to do and left God out completely!

God wants us to keep Him involved in everything we do. Good things come from choosing kindness and God's way. The best part of following God is knowing He sees everything and wants what's best for us.

David writes a song at the end of the book telling us that God's way is *perfect*. That's a very good reason to follow Him, even when we're tempted to think we know what's best for us. You make little decisions every day, like what to eat for breakfast, what shoes you'll wear, and who you'll sit with at lunch. But there will be some days when bigger decisions come along. A good habit to get into is asking God at the *beginning* of the day to help you make good choices. That way, you welcome Him to be a part of every choice you make.

BIG QUESTIONS

1. When you have a day that doesn't go the way you wanted it to, how do you talk to God about it?

2. When you have a really good day, how do you talk to God about it?

WORDS AND WISDOM TO SHARE

Get together with your family or friends and give everyone a piece of paper and pen or pencil. Ask everyone to make a list with two columns. Label one column "Haughty Heart" and the other "Humble Heart." In each column, list a time you had a haughty heart or a humble heart. Then have everyone talk about ways you can grow your humble heart.

WEEK #11

Learn to Listen

DAILY READINGS & REFLECTIONS

Day 1: Meet Solomon (from 1 Kings 3:5–15).
When Solomon became king, he asked God to give him a heart that could tell right from wrong. God was pleased by his request; He wants to see us make the right choices.

Day 2: Read 1 Kings 4:29–34.
Solomon prayed for wisdom and received more than anyone on earth! Ask God for wisdom, then see all He can do.

Day 3: "Solomon stood before the altar of the Lord...and said: 'Lord, the God of Israel, there is no God like you in heaven above or on earth below.'" (from 1 Kings 8:22–23)
Sharing our love for God, and our faith in Him, is a brave act.

Day 4: Meet Elijah (from 1 Kings 17).
Elijah was a prophet who saw God do amazing things. But he also had times of doubt. God doesn't expect us to be perfect all the time, but to remember He is always with us.

Day 5: Read 1 Kings 18:16–39.
One of Elijah's most notable miracles was to prove God's power and authority to the people of Israel and to the many prophets of the false god Baal.

Day 6: Read 1 Kings 19:1–14.
Following God's way is not always the easy or popular path. But we have God standing beside us in every challenge.

Day 7: "But Jehoshaphat also said to the king of Israel, 'First seek the counsel of the Lord.'" (from 1 Kings 22:5)
Put God first every day. Ask for guidance, give thanks, or sit with God in silence.

In the first book of Kings, we see what good listeners prophets had to be. Prophets were called to be direct lines from God to kings and the people under their rule. They relayed wisdom, warnings, and the interpretation of dreams. We can learn to hear and listen to God as well. Being a good listener is important in *all* our relationships—with God, our parents, friends, teachers, pastors, and even people we've just met.

Listening takes practice. When we spend time with a group of friends, it's hard to listen to everyone else's opinions or stories before we speak. We get eager to share what we have to say! But waiting to talk allows us to truly *hear* what our friends are saying, and that helps us understand one another better.

Becoming a good listener earns you respect, too, and encourages people to trust you. It shows you care. It makes others feel like they matter. It's another way to spread God's love in the world.

BIG QUESTIONS

1. God listens closely when you pray. Are you a good listener? How do you listen closely when He talks to you?

2. Have you ever doubted God? How did that feel? How did you overcome your doubt?

WORDS AND WISDOM TO SHARE

Invite your friends or family to do a listening exercise with you. Give everyone some paper and a pen or pencil. One at a time, have each person share a little story about their day with the group. When each person is finished talking, have everyone write down what they *heard*. Then take turns sharing what you heard, and compare it to what the speaker said.

WEEK #12

Looking for Miracles

DAILY READINGS & REFLECTIONS

Day 1: Read 2 Kings 2:1–18.
Elijah went to heaven in a whirlwind, swept up by chariots and horsemen. Elisha, his successor, saw it all. There are miracles to see in God's creation, if we pay attention.

Day 2: Read 2 Kings 4:1–7.
Elisha became a powerful prophet and performed many miracles for the people.

Day 3: Meet Naaman (from 2 Kings 5).
Naaman needed a miracle of healing. He was upset by the instructions the prophet Elisha gave him, but when he obeyed, he was healed.

Day 4: "They imitated the nations around them although the Lord had ordered them, 'Do not do as they do.'" (from 2 Kings 17:15)
Following the crowd can feel good. But going against what is right leads us away from God.

Day 5: Read 2 Kings 20:1–6.
Remember that God hears our prayers and sees every tear we cry, even when we're alone. God's love is wrapped around us like a hug that never ends!

Day 6: Meet Josiah (from 2 Kings 22:1–2).
Josiah became king when he was eight years old. His heart was determined not to turn away from God. At any age, you can decide to put God first.

Day 7: "Neither before nor after Josiah was there a king like him who turned to the Lord as he did—with all his heart and with all his soul and with all his strength." (from 2 Kings 23:25)
God asks us to stay close to Him with every part of who we are.

The second book of Kings is filled with miracles. Our world is *still* full of God's miracles waiting for us to see them. To begin with, *you're* a miracle! The fact that you are *one of a kind* in a world of eight billion people is amazing. You are part of the miracle of God's perfect timing. Whenever you feel alone or unsure, remember that God made you with careful attention and intention. He created you *on purpose*. Keep your eyes open to see God's miracles around you.

God loves to let us know how close He is, and that He's watching us intently. When a brightly colored bird flies by, or a rabbit hops in front of us, or a deer stops to stare, think of those as "winks" from God. It's His way of saying hello. When we hear the wind in the trees, a trickling stream, or the big sound that the crashing ocean waves make—all of it points us to the wonder of God. He loves when we notice that He's with us.

BIG QUESTIONS

1. How do you see God in the world around you every day? Are these "winks"?

2. How would you thank God for a miracle?

GOD AND ME

Reading about God's great miracles can make us feel small because His power is so awesome. Take some time to write about how these great miracles make you feel. What would you do if you'd been there to see them happen?

WEEK #13
The Power of Faith

DAILY READINGS & REFLECTIONS

Day 1: "He answered their prayers, because they trusted in Him." (from 1 Chronicles 5:20)
It feels good to have people in our life we can trust. You can *always* trust God. Your faith moves God to do big things.

Day 2: Read 1 Chronicles 6:31–32.
Music has always been an important part of worshipping God. It's a powerful way to be close to God and deepen our faith.

Day 3: Meet Joab (from 1 Chronicles 11:4–9).
Joab was loyal, brave, and ambitious. But he acted for approval, not because his actions were right. Stay faithful to God.

Day 4: Read 1 Chronicles 16:8–36.
In David's time, writing poetry and songs was a way to **exalt** God. Journaling about God's goodness is one way we can communicate our love for Him.

Day 5: Read 1 Chronicles 17:1–15.
Nathan was a prophet who had to deliver some disappointing news to David. Remember, if one plan fails, God is moving things around to make a *better* plan succeed.

Day 6: Read 1 Chronicles 28:2–10.
David told Solomon that if he searched for God, he would find Him. Faith is believing we can look for God and find Him in every part of our lives.

Day 7: "I know, my God, that You test the heart and are pleased with integrity." (from 1 Chronicles 29:17)
God uses different situations to test our hearts. Trust in Him.

The first book of Chronicles is about building faith. God showed His might through the trust of His people. King David understood that God tests our faith and is pleased with honest, determined devotion. We might expect something we prayed for, only to feel let down when we don't get it. When that happens, we have a chance to stand firm in our faith. Pushing through our disappointment with a good attitude lets God know we trust Him—and we *know* He wants what's best for us.

Imagine there's someone at school who is having a birthday party, and you are one of the only people in your class who isn't invited. That's a tough thing to accept. But what if, instead of getting angry, you trust God to help you? You can choose kindness and wish that person a happy birthday. You can share what you're going through with a parent and do something together that day.

Our faith gets more solid every time we turn to God in a hard situation. As our faith strengthens, God can use us to do bigger things than we ever thought possible.

BIG QUESTIONS

1. We can't see God physically, but having faith is seeing that He is always there. Can you think of a way you've seen God work in your life this week?

2. When have you had to lean on your faith to get through a hard time? How did you feel after?

WORDS AND WISDOM TO SHARE

Make a list of people who inspire your faith. The next time you see them or talk on the phone, tell them about your journey of faith!

WEEK #14

A Star for God's Honor

DAILY READINGS & REFLECTIONS

Day 1: Read 2 Chronicles 2:5–16.
Solomon was called to build a temple for God, and he wanted to do an excellent job. We honor God when we do our best work.

Day 2: "If My people, who are called by My name, will humble themselves and pray and seek My face...then I will hear from heaven." (from 2 Chronicles 7:14)
God wants to hear from you in prayer.

Day 3: Meet Asa (from 2 Chronicles 14:1–11).
Asa followed God's rules and ways, and he honored God and the people around him through prayer. God has a soft heart for those who seek Him in prayer.

Day 4: "For the eyes of the Lord range throughout the earth to strengthen those whose hearts are fully committed to Him." (from 2 Chronicles 16:9)
God is constantly watching over you to make you strong.

Day 5: Read 2 Chronicles 20:1–19.
King Jehoshaphat called out to God: "We do not know what to do, but our eyes are on You." God doesn't want you to be afraid. Be honest in prayer and He will guide you.

Day 6: Meet Uzziah (from 2 Chronicles 26).
Things went well for Uzziah for many years before he dishonored God. We'll never "get away" with something we know is wrong.

Day 7: "In everything that he undertook...he sought his God and worked wholeheartedly. And so he prospered." (from 2 Chronicles 31:21)
When we love and honor God, we open our life to His greatest blessings.

The second book of Chronicles covers kings and kingdoms, and how good things happen to those who honor God. Since creation, God has told His people that honoring and obeying Him leads to a blessed life. They rebelled, strayed, and made many mistakes. But they discovered God's love *never* runs out.

Acting honorably is a big part of loving God. When you find something that doesn't belong to you, or a classmate asks you to let them copy your answers on a test, or someone encourages you to talk behind a friend's back, you know the right way to respond. When God's love is in your heart, His spirit guides you. We won't be perfect in all our actions, but when we slip, God is there to pick us up with love and forgiveness.

Every day is a new chance to honor God with our choices. When we do, we inspire our friends to do the same. It creates a domino effect of honesty, courage, and kindness. You become a star that shines in the *best* possible way.

BIG QUESTIONS

1. Can you think of a few ways to honor God in your life today?

2. What can you do this week to show your firm commitment to God?

GOD AND ME

Your relationship with God is personal to you, but God wants you to share His love with others. How do you feel when you talk to other people about God? Are there people you could talk to so that you can grow closer to Him?

WEEK #15

Hitting the Restart Button

DAILY READINGS & REFLECTIONS

Day 1: "Everyone whose heart God had moved—prepared to go up and build the house of the Lord in Jerusalem." (from Ezra 1:5)
God "moves" our heart to do what honors Him.

Day 2: Read Ezra 3:10–13.
God's people were filled with emotion when the temple's foundation was laid, and their hearts returned to God. God will *always* make ways to help us through our bumpy days.

Day 3: "Then the peoples around them set out to discourage the people of Judah and make them afraid to go on building." (from Ezra 4:4)
Some people treat others in ways God would never want. Remember to be kind.

Day 4: Meet King Darius (from Ezra 6:1–12).
King Darius supported God's people in rebuilding the temple. When good things happen, we know they came from God—and He might send them in a surprising way.

Day 5: Meet Ezra (from Ezra 7:6–10).
Ezra was an important part of leading the Israelites to **repent** and restore their relationship with God. Being quick to forgive is the way to God giving us a clean slate.

Day 6: Read Ezra 7:27–28.
God changed the heart of a king to bring favor to His people. God's love shapes a person's heart. We can take any problem to Him, and He will work to help us start again.

Day 7: "I proclaimed a fast, so that we might humble ourselves before our God and ask Him for a safe journey for us and our children." (from Ezra 8:21)
We can always ask God for help. Every gift is from Him.

The book of Ezra is about having the courage to start over. The Israelites who had been driven into exile were allowed to return to Jerusalem to rebuild God's temple. Ezra praised God because He "put it into the king's heart to bring honor to the house of the Lord in Jerusalem this way" (Ezra 7:27). God's compassion for His people never paused. His forgiveness is part of the never-ending story of His love for us.

When you make a mistake, guilt can cause you to shy away from talking to God. But God's arms are always open wide, inviting you to stay close. Nothing you do can keep Him from loving you. If you talk to God when you feel sorry about something you've done, like disobeying your parents, saying unkind words to a friend, or talking badly about a fellow classmate, God forgives you. He wants you to know you can start over. Each time you do, your heart learns to offer others the same kindness.

BIG QUESTIONS

1. Is it hard for you to put mistakes behind you? How can you ask God to help you move forward more easily?

2. Are you able to forgive others quickly or is it difficult for you? Why do you think that is?

3. Learning from our mistakes makes us wiser. What lessons has God shown you in a mistake you've made? How did learning from that mistake make you more kind?

WORDS AND WISDOM TO SHARE

We see fresh starts everywhere in God's creation—when trees lose their leaves and become green again, when flowers fade and new blooms form, and *every* morning when the sun comes up. Ask a parent to help you buy flower bulbs or seeds to plant. Over the next few weeks, observe your flower grow into a beautiful bloom. Every time you look at it, ask God to be with you as you bloom and start over, too.

GOD AND ME

God wants you to remember that when you pick yourself up after making a mistake, He's there to help you stand tall again. Draw a picture of yourself that shows how proud you feel when God is standing beside you.

WEEK #16

With God, It's Possible!

DAILY READINGS & REFLECTIONS

Day 1: Meet Nehemiah (from Nehemiah 1).

Nehemiah was **cupbearer** to the king. He needed the king's approval to help the Israelites—so God made it possible.

Day 2: "The king said to me, 'What is it you want?' Then I prayed to the God of heaven, and I answered the king." (from Nehemiah 2:4–5)

You can always send a prayer from your heart to heaven—and trust God will answer.

Day 3: Read Nehemiah 4:1–6.

It isn't always easy to follow God when you're with others who don't know or trust Him. But if you follow God, you might convince others to do the same.

Day 4: "All the surrounding nations were afraid... They realized that this work had been done with the help of our God." (from Nehemiah 6:16)

You can do anything you put your mind to. All things are possible with God.

Day 5: Meet Hanani (from Nehemiah 7:1–2).

Hanani held a deep respect for God and was put in charge of the newly built gates of Jerusalem. Every act of service should be done in a way that respects God.

Day 6: "The joy of the Lord is your strength." (from Nehemiah 8:10)

Joy comes from knowing God loves you, celebrates you, and values you every day. It's possible to stand up against anything when you keep joy in your heart.

Day 7: Read Nehemiah 9:6–8.

God gives life to everything and makes anything possible—even your wildest dreams.

The book of Nehemiah is about possibilities. When Nehemiah heard that the walls of Jerusalem were broken down and the Israelites were in trouble, he sat and cried. Then he prayed. God heard Nehemiah's request, and made it possible for him to rebuild the city of his ancestors. Nehemiah wasn't sure it was going to go as well as it did. The Bible says he was "very much afraid" (Nehemiah 2:2). We've all felt that way—nervous and afraid—when we face an impossible task. With God's help, Nehemiah was able to do the right thing with courage in his heart.

God gives us the confidence to do what is in front of us. Even when something feels incredibly hard, God helps us, one step at a time.

What you think is hard might be easy for your friend or sibling. That can be upsetting. But the things *you* do well are the things that make you special—and the same goes for them. Our unique gifts make the world a better place, and God planned it that way.

BIG QUESTIONS

1. What brings you joy?

2. Can you think of something you've had to do that made you feel "very much afraid," like Nehemiah felt? How did you find the courage to do it?

3. What is something you dream of doing that seems kind of impossible?

WORDS AND WISDOM TO SHARE

Sit with a friend and make a list of some of your daily tasks and activities. Note which tasks are hard or easy for each of you. Then work through each of the hard tasks together to come up with some ways you can support each other.

GOD AND ME

Write a prayer to God, listing the things you hope to do one day. God will shape your hopes and dreams as you grow, but the ideas that are in your heart right now matter. Make sure to tell Him about the big things that seem out of reach—He's big enough to make *those* hopes and dreams come true, too.

WEEK #17
All for a Purpose

DAILY READINGS & REFLECTIONS

Day 1: Meet Esther (from Esther 2:5–18).
Esther lost her parents when she was young, and was raised by her cousin. God puts families together in different ways.

Day 2: Meet Mordecai (from Esther 2:19–22).
Mordecai took Esther in as a daughter, and he brought her up with wisdom and godliness. Esther played a valuable part in the purpose God had for both of them.

Day 3: Read Esther 3:1–13.
God gave Esther a position that allowed her to save the Israelites from a terrible plan. If there is something God wants us to do, He will make a way to get it done.

Day 4: Read Esther 4:1–17.
When Esther realized God had a brave and special purpose for her, she called on her people to pray. Prayer will boost your courage in whatever you are facing.

Day 5: "Haman…robed Mordecai, and led him on horseback through the city streets, proclaiming…, 'This is what is done for the man the king delights to honor!'" (from Esther 6:11)
God knew that Haman plotted to destroy Mordecai. But God worked it out so that Mordecai was honored. God honors those who love Him.

Day 6: "The king's edict granted the Jews in every city the right to assemble and protect themselves." (from Esther 8:11)
God's purpose for Mordecai and Esther was bigger than they could have known. God's purpose for you will be bigger than you know, too.

Day 7: Read Esther 10:3.
God gives us the courage to speak up in defense of those who are treated unfairly. God will use your bravery for good.

The book of Esther shows how fully you can trust God's plan. God had a purpose for Esther that went beyond what she could have dreamed. She was crowned queen at a young age, and boldly saved the lives of the Jewish people from Haman's cruel plan.

The plans God has for you are good. The purposes you fulfill will bring you success and honor Him. There are countless ways for God to bless the world through you. You might work at an animal shelter, help at a food bank, or do something to show appreciation for others. God's purpose for you isn't just one thing—it's a collection of *all* the things you do to bring God's love and goodness to the world.

Sometimes you might get discouraged because you let your loved ones down or do something you aren't proud of. But you can't let stumbles keep you from staying on the path of your good purpose. Even when plans fail, God's purpose won't fade. You shine His light every time you have the courage to follow what's right. Your purpose is as special as *you* are.

BIG QUESTIONS

1. Esther didn't know the purpose God had for her before she became queen. She trusted God one day at a time. How do you trust God each and every day?

2. How did you honor God this week with good deeds?

3. Make a list of the things you do to bring God's love and goodness to the world. Then, the next time you pray, remember to thank Him for those gifts.

WORDS AND WISDOM TO SHARE

Gather some family members or some friends and make a "Right Way Plan." Ask everyone to think of a time they chose the right thing when it wasn't easy, and what helped them in that moment. Write down the qualities or actions to take when you need to choose the right way. Then make a promise to your friends, family, and God that you'll follow the Right Way.

GOD AND ME

Close your eyes and picture yourself doing what you dream of doing. Draw a picture of yourself standing beside God in your purpose, fulfilling your dreams.

WEEK #18

What If We Don't Understand?

DAILY READINGS & REFLECTIONS

Day 1: Meet Job (from Job 1).
Job was a man who loved God. Even when he lost everything, he refused to blame God. God will never leave us alone. He's the One we can depend on.

Day 2: "No one said a word to him, because they saw how great his suffering was." (from Job 2:13)
It's important to show the people we care about that we're thinking of them and will be there in their time of need.

Day 3: Meet Eliphaz (from Job 4:7–8).
Eliphaz assumed Job was being punished by God for something he did. But Eliphaz shouldn't have judged. God alone sees our heart.

Day 4: Read Job 32:1–9.
Elihu was the youngest to speak to Job, but the wisest of them all. Your decision to follow God when you're young means you can start changing the world now.

Day 5: "Those who suffer He delivers in their suffering; He speaks to them in their affliction." (from Job 36:15)
In our life, there are trials and suffering we don't understand. But God is always with us.

Day 6: Read Job 38:1–7.
Sometimes, like Job, we want to question God or feel sorry for ourselves for the things that are happening in our lives. God stays with us while we are hurting.

Day 7: Read Job 42:10–17.
God restored Job's wealth and gave him even more than he had before his time of suffering. Don't give up on God's goodness.

The book of Job is about suffering in life, and responding in faith. Job lost everything. But his immediate reaction reflected his trust in God. In time, he did become angry. He felt his suffering was unfair. Even when we don't understand the reason bad things happen, blame and anger don't help us. God is with us at all times, and the Bible says He's especially close to those who are suffering.

When we hear about natural disasters like wildfires and hurricanes, it can make us feel upset or afraid. Praying is something we can do to release those feelings. God is the comfort in our pain and the peace in our fear. We can ask Him to be with those who are going through a difficult time. If something happens in our town or neighborhood, we can also get involved. Actively helping others helps our hearts heal. There might be people in need of hot meals, water, clothing, or a helping hand to clean up. You and your family can decide how you can share God's love with others.

BIG QUESTIONS

1. What helps you to trust God when bad things happen?

2. The world is full of things we don't understand. Instead of asking, "Why did this happen?" how can you respond to show your faith in God?

WORDS AND WISDOM TO SHARE

The next time you're with friends, ask if anyone is going through something that's hard to understand. Talk about how you can pray for one another and support one another. Consider other ways you can help one another, too, and make a plan to do them.

WEEK #19

Being Thankful

DAILY READINGS & REFLECTIONS

Day 1: "In peace I will lie down and sleep, for You alone, Lord, make me dwell in safety." (from Psalm 4:8)
At the end of each day, we can rest knowing that God holds our worries so we can find peace.

Day 2: Read Psalm 8.
It can be hard to see how special you are. But if you ever lose sight of your worth, remember that God has "crowned [you] with glory and honor."

Day 3: Read Psalm 23.
When we're nervous about an upcoming event or we've had a not-so-good day, God is there to comfort us.

Day 4: Meet Asaph (Psalm 73).
Asaph, the author of this Psalm, was a Levite singer, prophet, and poet. Music was an important part of the culture in Biblical times and still brings us closer to God.

Day 5: Meet Ethan (Psalm 89).
Ethan was known for his wisdom. He was a leader of temple music and wrote Psalm 89. Our special gifts are woven into us by God's hand when He creates us.

Day 6: Read Psalm 91.
God commands His angels to protect you. You have your own guardian angels, and they pay close attention to keep you safe.

Day 7: "I praise You because I am fearfully and wonderfully made; Your works are wonderful, I know that full well." (from Psalm 139:14)
Always remember the way *God* describes you: wonderful, amazing, marvelous.

The book of Psalms is the longest book in the Bible. It has 150 chapters! It's a collection of poems, prayers, and songs written by different people. David wrote more than anyone else. The poems include praise for God's miracles. They express His people's emotions during times of struggle. And they give hope for the promise of a coming Savior.

Writing about how we feel is a good way to process the things we go through. It can help us see how we should pray and what we need help with. Maybe we're too quick to speak when we get mad. Maybe we have trouble listening to directions. Maybe we lose our patience. Because we're not perfect, we have some *very* good things to be thankful for every day: God's love, kindness, patience, and forgiveness.

Being thankful is a strategy for joy. When we shift our focus from problems to praise, we learn that thanking God for what He's done opens the door to more blessings.

BIG QUESTIONS

1. Thankfulness changes your perspective, creating a happier, more positive you! Can you think of two things you're thankful for today?

2. Music is a gift from God. We feel God's love and presence when we sing songs of praise. Do you have a favorite song you like to sing to God?

3. How do you feel when you complain? How do you feel when you're grateful? Can you write down the differences?

WORDS AND WISDOM TO SHARE

Suggest a family sing-along night. Have everyone choose a song of worship. It can be any style of music. Dancing and playing an instrument are welcome, too! Celebrate with joy, and talk about the things God has done for you and why you're thankful.

GOD AND ME

In Psalm 9:1, David wrote, "I will give thanks to You, Lord, with all my heart; I will tell of all Your wonderful deeds." Write a psalm like David did, in your own words, thanking God.

WEEK #20

A Book of Wisdom

DAILY READINGS & REFLECTIONS

Day 1: "The fear of the Lord is the beginning of knowledge." (from Proverbs 1:7)
Having an awe-inspiring respect for God opens our heart to wisdom.

Day 2: Read Proverbs 3:27–30.
Being a good friend or a good neighbor means being generous, kind, thoughtful, and honest. These qualities create good relationships—and we should not hold them back.

Day 3: "Above all else, guard your heart, for everything you do flows from it." (from Proverbs 4:23)
Think of your heart as a house that holds everything you love. God will help you protect it.

Day 4: "The righteous choose their friends carefully, but the way of the wicked leads them astray." (from Proverbs 12:26)
Having a good friend is a blessing. Ask God to give you friends who encourage your growth.

Day 5: Read Proverbs 15–17.
There are 94 pieces of wisdom in these three chapters. It's like digging up buried treasure from King Solomon, the wisest man who ever lived.

Day 6: Read Proverbs 22:1–6.
Don't make hasty decisions, honor God for a rewarding life, watch out for those who lead you into wrongdoing, and remember what you've learned as you get older.

Day 7: "Pride brings a person low, but the lowly in spirit gain honor." (from Proverbs 29:23)
God created everyone with *infinite* worth.

The book of Proverbs is a book of wisdom. King Solomon is given credit for writing most of the proverbs, which are short sayings filled with good advice. This is a good book to read again and again as you learn to follow God. The verses are easy to memorize. They can become a collection of guidance you carry around with you.

God is generous when giving wisdom to those who ask for it. When we have a decision to make and we're not sure what to do, it's best to pray first. God knows how it will turn out, so He's always the right one to ask. Maybe you've been asked to join a study group, but when you did, you found out it was more of a gossip group. You might struggle with whether to go back to the group and stand up for what's right, or remove yourself from the group entirely. That's a good time to talk to God—and you might ask your parents to pray with you, too. You'll know in your heart what you should do.

BIG QUESTIONS

1. Think about a mistake you've made and what you learned from it. Is there a little wisdom you could make into a proverb?

2. Think of something that happened this week that you wish you'd handled differently. What would you do if you had a do-over?

3. God uses your parents and the grown-ups you trust to give you guidance and wisdom. What is some good advice they've given to you lately? How have you put it into practice?

WORDS AND WISDOM TO SHARE

Get a few friends together and exchange helpful advice you've heard. Each of you can write down your "bit of wisdom" on note cards and trade. Choose your favorite verses from the book of Proverbs and share those, too. Then carry the note cards with you to remember your friends, their wisdom, and God's love.

GOD AND ME

Write down some things you struggle with and ask God for the wisdom to handle them.

WEEK #21

Living Happily!

DAILY READINGS & REFLECTIONS

Day 1: "The sun rises and the sun sets, and hurries back to where it rises." (from Ecclesiastes 1:5)

Time passes very quickly. Following God and being thankful helps us make the most of our days.

Day 2: "To the person who pleases Him, God gives wisdom, knowledge and happiness." (from Ecclesiastes 2:26)

God gives us everything that makes our life better.

Day 3: Read Ecclesiastes 3:9–14.

Our days are in God's hands—even days that don't go the way we want. You can grumble and sulk, or you can choose a good attitude, trusting that God will work everything together for your good.

Day 4: Read Ecclesiastes 4:9–12.

Friends are important. God created us with a desire for companionship—starting with our relationship with Him. Being close to God makes us a better friend.

Day 5: Read Ecclesiastes 5:18–20.

Believe it or not, schoolwork, chores, and other work are gifts from God! Be thankful for your teachers, your home, and the ability to do a job well.

Day 6: "The quiet words of the wise are more to be heeded than the shouts of a ruler of fools." (from Ecclesiastes 9:17)

Wisdom doesn't always come from people in high places—God often gives it quietly, through those with humble hearts.

Day 7: Read Ecclesiastes 12.

You are loved more than you'll ever know. When we trust God with our whole heart, our days hold more happiness and our world more wonder than we're able to contain.

Like Proverbs, the book of Ecclesiastes is a book of wisdom. It talks about being happy with the life God gives us. Sometimes you might want to skip the growing-up process and just be a *grown-up*. But every day is a gift from God. When you open your eyes in the morning, know that God is ready to start the day with you. You don't have to worry about how it will go. Instead, think about *who* is going with you! God wants you to call on Him whenever you need to. Together, you'll tackle whatever is ahead, from scuffles with friends to a test you ace.

God knows you'll have days that are difficult, frustrating, and even sad. Ups and downs are part of life. Learning to trust God no matter what is how we get through our days—in a peaceful, hopeful, and happier way! As soon as you wake up, thank God for two things. During your day, do one kind deed. Before the end of your day, read, laugh, clean your room, tell your parents you appreciate them, or hug a sibling or friend. When you make up your mind to have a good day, the happy days start adding up.

BIG QUESTIONS

1. What helpful or kind thing do you do that makes you feel happy?

2. When is it hardest for you to be positive and thankful? Have you asked God to help you?

WORDS AND WISDOM TO SHARE

Get together with your family and have each person write down ten things that make them happy and thankful. Start your lists with, "My name is ______________, God loves me, and this is what makes me happy and thankful." Talk about your lists and what you learned about one another.

WEEK #22

The Desire of Our Heart

DAILY READINGS & REFLECTIONS

Day 1: "We rejoice and delight in you; we will praise your love." (from Song of Songs 1:4)
When you like someone, you think about them a lot. When we think of God this way, the hopes in our heart grow.

Day 2: Read Song of Songs 2.
Longing for something means we can hardly wait for it to happen! That's how God feels about spending time with us. He looks forward to it, and rejoices when it happens.

Day 3: "I will search for the one my heart loves." (from Song of Songs 3:2)
Loving God means wanting to get to know Him.

Day 4: "Awake, north wind, and come, south wind! Blow on my garden, that its fragrance may spread everywhere." (from Song of Songs 4:16)
When we show God's love to others, we are like the wind, spreading the knowledge of His goodness everywhere.

Day 5: "This is my beloved, this is my friend." (from Song of Songs 5:16)
God called Abraham His friend. God talked to Moses as a friend. God is your friend, too.

Day 6: "Who is this that appears like the dawn, fair as the moon, bright as the sun, majestic as the stars?" (from Song of Songs 6:10)
All of creation expresses the glory of God.

Day 7: "Many waters cannot quench love; rivers cannot sweep it away." (from Song of Songs 8:7)
God's love for you stands strong. It can't be watered down or washed away.

Song of Songs is a collection of poems written by a couple in love and their friends. The book is considered an **allegory** for the love and desire we have for God. God fulfills our heart's desire for a love that won't fail. His love is perfect. There is no one else as patient, kind, or forgiving.

Your life is full of people and things you love. God fills your life with good things because He loves *you*. When our heart's desire is to love God, His love becomes our biggest influence. If you struggle with being nice to your siblings or holding in unkind words, getting closer to God will help you. In time, your actions and words will become more loving, kind, and patient.

What we want most is up to us. What we desire most will influence everything we do. When we put God first, we put ourselves in the most loving place we can be.

BIG QUESTIONS

1. The next time someone upsets you, how can you react in a loving way?

2. Love is always kind. Can you remember a few ways you've shown your love through kindness this week?

WORDS AND WISDOM TO SHARE

With your family, decide to do some things to spread God's love. Make a meal for a neighbor. Take cookies to a nursing home. Write thank-you cards to your teachers. Volunteer to pick up litter or do yard work for an elderly neighbor. Or come up with something unique to your family and neighborhood.

WEEK #23

Waiting Patiently

DAILY READINGS & REFLECTIONS

Day 1: Meet Isaiah (from Isaiah 1).
Isaiah was a prophet known for the clear prediction of the coming of Jesus (the **Messiah**), and his message of hope for God's people.

Day 2: Read Isaiah 9:1–7.
Isaiah talks about a big thing the world is waiting for: the coming of Jesus, our Savior and King. God's greatest gifts come while we wait.

Day 3: "Lord…You have done wonderful things, things planned long ago." (from Isaiah 25:1)
You won't always understand why it takes so long for things to happen, or why they sometimes don't happen at all, but God does.

Day 4: Meet Hezekiah (from Isaiah 36–37).
Hezekiah had to wait for word from God while he was in great distress. God wants us to give our worries to Him while we wait to see how things will work out.

Day 5: Read Isaiah 40:25–31.
God names every star in the sky. He's a heavenly Father who pays attention to detail and understands us better than anyone else.

Day 6: "I am the Lord your God, who teaches you what is best for you, who directs you in the way you should go." (from Isaiah 48:17)
God knows what's best for you. He'll show you the way.

Day 7: "You, Lord, are our Father. We are the clay, You are the potter; we are all the work of Your hand." (from Isaiah 64:8)
You are God's masterpiece. He's shaping your heart and preparing you for *so many* good things.

The book of Isaiah is about hoping for the good things God has planned, and trusting Him while we wait. Learning to be patient is hard. It takes practice. Holding our tongue when we get mad, believing God loves us when we don't get what we want, and trusting that His choices are the best ones for us—*all* of these challenges test our patience.

The gift God gives to help us while we wait is *hope*. Hope keeps us positive. Hope lifts us up when we start to feel down. God tells us in Isaiah 49:23, "Those who hope in Me will not be disappointed." Knowing God's plan for us is good, no matter how we feel, is how we stay hopeful.

God knit you together with care and detail. From the moment you were born, His love has shaped you. God protects you from harm. He gives you wise counsel. He picks you up when you fall. He carries you when you're weak. His love is constant and eternal. These are the things you should repeat to yourself on your hardest days. Just *wait and see* the good things to come when you keep trusting God.

BIG QUESTIONS

1. Is it hard for you to wait patiently? What do you think might help you get better at it?

2. God takes care of every detail of your life. What has He done that makes you feel most confident about waiting for His best plans?

3. Hope is a feeling of excitement for the good things God has in store, even though we're not sure when they'll happen. What are you hoping for?

WORDS AND WISDOM TO SHARE

Ask some of your friends or your family to sit with you and pray for the things you're hoping for. You can ask everyone to write down their biggest hopes and collect them in a jar or basket that you set in the center of your group.

GOD AND ME

Learning to trust God takes time. Waiting for prayers to be answered is challenging. Write down your questions for God about His timing. Is there something you wanted to see happen that didn't, or something you wished happened more quickly? Getting to know God will help you understand His plan.

WEEK #24

Speak Up!

DAILY READINGS & REFLECTIONS

Day 1: Meet Jeremiah (from Jeremiah 1:1–17).
Jeremiah was called to be a prophet to the nations. He thought he was too young to speak to others. You are never too young to speak up for what is right.

Day 2: Read Jeremiah 10:1–25.
God's people stopped speaking up for God's commandments, and they began to forget God's love. Putting God first makes us, and our world, more kind.

Day 3: Read Jeremiah 17:7–8.
When we put our trust and confidence in God, we speak the truth with courage, help others with compassion, and give to the poor with generosity.

Day 4: "I will give them a heart to know me… They will be my people, and I will be their God." (from Jeremiah 24:7)
When we serve God, our lives become a collection of good choices and good deeds.

Day 5: "'For I know the plans I have for you,' declares the Lord, 'plans to prosper you and not to harm you, plans to give you hope and a future.'" (from Jeremiah 29:11)
Trust that God is leading you every day.

Day 6: "This is what the Lord says… 'Call to Me and I will answer you and tell you great and unsearchable things you do not know.'" (from Jeremiah 33:2–3)
You can call on God anytime, day or night, and know that He will always be there.

Day 7: Meet Baruch (from Jeremiah 36:1–10).
Baruch was a close friend of Jeremiah. He recorded stories about Jeremiah's life. Writing is a way of "speaking up" for good, true, and right things. Words are powerful.

This book begins with God asking Jeremiah the priest to be a prophet to the nations. Jeremiah was reluctant, but he obeyed God and used his voice to declare the truth. It's a brave thing to speak up. There were messages of warning and hope for a rebellious people who abandoned the commandments of God. One of the worst things they did was take advantage of the less fortunate. God's heart is tender toward those who are alone and need help.

You can speak up and encourage your friends to look for ways to help others. You can get together with your family and pray about what to do to improve the lives of those who are alone or hurting.

If there are kids at your school who are being treated wrongly, speaking up for them is a courageous kindness. Becoming their friend is an act of love. God puts compassion in our heart for the sake of others. Even small amounts of love can light up a school, a city, and a life.

BIG QUESTIONS

1. We "speak up" for kindness and love through our words and actions. In what ways would you like to speak up in your school and community?

2. How could you speak up for and defend someone who was being picked on at school, knowing that God is standing with you?

3. Do you feel nervous when you speak in front of others? What helps you be brave in those moments?

WORDS AND WISDOM TO SHARE

Invite a group of friends over and, with the help of your parents, choose some places in your community where you can actively participate to help others.

GOD AND ME

Prayer is the way we communicate with God. We can talk to Him about *anything*—our worries, disappointments, whatever we're sad or scared about, and whatever we need help figuring out! Write down a prayer for His guidance when you need to speak up for someone less fortunate than you.

WEEK #25
Let Your Feelings Flow

DAILY READINGS & REFLECTIONS

Day 1: "Pour out your heart like water in the presence of the Lord." (from Lamentations 2:19)
Pour out your heart in prayer. Nothing is too big or too small for God to help you.

Day 2: "His compassions never fail. They are new every morning; great is Your faithfulness." (from Lamentations 3:22–23)
When you wake up to a new day, all things are new in God's eyes.

Day 3: "The Lord is my portion; therefore I will wait for Him." (from Lamentations 3:24)
When the Bible says the Lord is our portion, it means He's our security, hope, and happiness. He's *everything* we need to live a blessed life.

Day 4: "The Lord is good to those whose hope is in Him, to the one who seeks Him." (from Lamentations 3:25)
Putting your hope in God is putting it in the best place it can be.

Day 5: "Let us lift up our hearts and our hands to God in heaven." (from Lamentations 3:41)
When we praise God, our hearts are filled with thankfulness.

Day 6: "You came near when I called You, and You said, 'Do not fear.'" (from Lamentations 3:57)
When you focus on how much God loves you, your fear is the first to go.

Day 7: "You, Lord, reign forever; Your throne endures from generation to generation." (from Lamentations 5:19)
God rules with love and gentleness. Everything He does begins with love.

The book of Lamentations is a collection of poems written by people expressing their emotions to God. To *lament* means to express sorrow or regret. Even though God sees our heart and knows our thoughts, He also listens when we speak. He gave us emotions, and He has them, too, because we're created to be like Him. He understands us completely!

One of the most valuable ways we can express our emotions is by telling God we're sorry for things we do that aren't loving or kind. There will be days when your feelings are hard to control. You might lose your temper with your sibling, or say something that offends a friend. Taking your emotions to God in prayer is a way to diffuse them. Talking to God about your feelings is a chance to be open and honest with Him and with yourself. It also helps you reach better understanding.

Prayer is kind of like a release valve for our feelings—it lets out the negative emotions and makes room for God to replace them with love and encouragement.

BIG QUESTIONS

1. Which emotion is hardest for you to control? Do you talk to God about it?

2. Who has God put in your life that you can talk to when you're feeling upset or sad?

GOD AND ME

Fill in these blanks:

God's love is higher than ______.

God's love is wider than ______.

God's love is deeper than ______.

WEEK #26
Seeking God

DAILY READINGS & REFLECTIONS

Day 1: **Meet Ezekiel (from Ezekiel 2).**
Ezekiel was a priest and prophet. He was surprised when God began to speak to him and show him visions. When God gives you a responsibility, He wants you to depend on Him.

Day 2: **"Listen carefully and take to heart all the words I speak to you." (from Ezekiel 3:10)**
Being a good listener makes us a good friend. Listening carefully to God makes us a good friend, too.

Day 3: **Read Ezekiel 11:14–25.**
God tells the Israelites He will give them an "undivided heart." That means they will seek Him first and serve Him alone.

Day 4: **"I will fulfill whatever I say, declares the Sovereign Lord." (from Ezekiel 12:25)**
When we keep our word we earn the respect of others and learn to trust.

Day 5: **"I will give you a new heart and put a new spirit in you." (from Ezekiel 36:26)**
God makes everything new. When our heart is broken, He stays near to mend it.

Day 6: **"I will put My Spirit in you and move you to follow My decrees and be careful to keep my laws." (from Ezekiel 36:27)**
Love becomes a part of who you are when you follow God.

Day 7: **"I will show My greatness and My holiness, and I will make Myself known in the sight of many nations." (from Ezekiel 38:23)**
God's love is a healing balm for the world. Be generous with others.

The prophet Ezekiel received vivid visions from God. They communicated God's message of disappointment and even anger over the sins of His people. The world is full of **temptations** to stray from God and do what seems best to us—or what we think will be *better* for us. The most important thing to remember is that God sees the entire reel of our life, from beginning to end. Following Him gives us the security of knowing *everything* goes through the filter of His love.

Have you ignored a rule at home or school, and suffered the consequence of it? That's the very thing God wants you to avoid. As a loving Father, He wants to see you succeed in everything you do. Mistakes happen, but when you make a mistake, get back up and keep following God. Ask Him what you can learn and how to do better. Let your heart feel sorry and even sad—but don't stay down.

Seeking God is the best decision you can make if you want to be a good student, a good friend, and a good force in the world. The light of God's love shines brightly through you when you let Him lead.

BIG QUESTIONS

1. God's love makes us new from the inside out. How have you been changed by learning to seek and follow His ways?

2. What are some ways you've shined the light of God's love in the world this week?

WISDOM AND WORD TO SHARE

Together with your family, make plans to light up your neighborhood with little acts of love. Is there a neighbor who hasn't been feeling well? Would they love some chicken noodle soup? Is there a friend near you who needs to feel included? Can you spend time with them?

WEEK #27

Hearts of Heavenly Courage

DAILY READINGS & REFLECTIONS

Day 1: Meet Daniel (from Daniel 1–2).
Daniel was a prophet and a high-ranking official in the king's court. God gave him the ability to interpret dreams and visions.

Day 2: Meet Shadrach, Meshach, and Abednego (from Daniel 3).
These three Jewish men were Daniel's friends. They also served in the king's court. They showed amazing bravery and trust in God over all else.

Day 3: Read Daniel 4:19–37.
King Nebuchadnezzar's pride drove him away from people for seven years!

Day 4: "Finally these men said, 'We will never find any basis for charges against this man Daniel unless it has something to do with the law of his God.'" (from Daniel 6:5)
Daniel's enemies were trying to get him into trouble with the king. But Daniel stood up for God's commandments without fear.

Day 5: Read Daniel 6:6–23.
Daniel was thrown into the lion's den because he refused to honor a king over God. Your heavenly courage will come at different times and for different reasons.

Day 6: "Do not be afraid, Daniel. Since the first day that you set your mind to gain understanding and to humble yourself before your God, your words were heard." (from Daniel 10:12)
Ask God for courage when you pray.

Day 7: "Those who are wise will shine like the brightness of the heavens." (from Daniel 12:3)
Let's pray that our lives become the light that shines for others.

The book of Daniel tells us about four men who were full of courage. Their love for God made them brave. Their trust in God made them bold in the face of *colossal* challenges—being thrown into a fiery furnace and a lion's den! Tests of our faith are very different now, but God hasn't changed. He still gives us the courage we need when we put our trust in Him.

We all get nervous or afraid sometimes. You might have a friend who loves to be first in line to try something new and you don't understand how they do it. Maybe you don't like speaking up in class or being called on to answer. When you feel fear building up inside you, that's the time to ask God for courage and trust Him to help you conquer your doubt. God is always with you. More than anything, He wants you to know you can count on Him for the strength, courage, and boldness you need.

BIG QUESTIONS

1. Is there something coming up in your life that you need courage for?

2. Daniel's faith was the size of a mountain and just as strong! How do you build your faith?

3. God uses our lives to lead others to Him. In what ways do you think He's using you to shine like the stars for other people?

WORDS AND WISDOM TO SHARE

Ask some friends to join you in discussing times you've put your trust in God to be brave. Talk about how He helped you and how your faith grew because of it. What can you learn from one another?

GOD AND ME

Sometimes, no matter how much courage we think we have, the mountain in front of us seems impossible to climb. Is it hard for you to trust God in these moments? Why do you think that is? What can you do to change that?

WEEK #28

Compassion for Others

DAILY READINGS & REFLECTIONS

Day 1: Meet Hosea (from Hosea 1).

Hosea was a prophet. His story makes clear that God is **long-suffering** with His people. His punishment for their sin is just, and His compassion leads to forgiveness.

Day 2: "I will show My love to the one I called 'Not My loved one.' I will say to those called 'Not My people,' 'You are My people'.'" (from Hosea 2:23)

God knows how it feels to be rejected. Still, He forgives.

Day 3: Read Hosea 6:1–3.

Sometimes what we hope for falls apart, and we're disappointed. God keeps our hope alive like spring rains restore the earth. He makes everything new again!

Day 4: Meet Ephraim (from Hosea 11:1–11).

Hosea referred to the people of the Northern Kingdom of Israel as *Ephraim*. God talks about them as if they are His children because God is our Heavenly Father.

Day 5: "But you must return to your God; maintain love and justice, and wait for your God always." (from Hosea 12:6)

When your patience runs thin, try to think about how kind God is with us.

Day 6: Read Hosea 14:1–8.

The Israelites turned from their wrongdoing and found God filled with mercy. Showing compassion after being disrespected is hard. But it will *always* bring the greater reward.

Day 7: "The ways of the Lord are right; the righteous walk in them, but the rebellious stumble in them." (from Hosea 14:9)

When we stay close to God, He guides our steps to what is best.

Hosea is a book about the Israelite's disloyalty to God, and God's unstoppable compassion for them. God won't stop loving us no matter how many mistakes we make. Imagine walking down a trail covered with rocks and fallen branches. Now picture God clearing the way to keep you from getting hurt or tripping over harmful things. That's what happens when we stay close to Him.

When we feel sad about things we see in the world, it's because we have a compassionate heart like God. It hurts us to know people have lost their home in a natural disaster, to learn about a child who is fighting an illness, or to see a stray animal that hasn't been treated well. We begin to understand the way God's heart hurts when we're hurting.

Compassion toward people, animals, and even the natural world reveals the love of God *within* us. It should move us into action! When we're able to ease the suffering we see, even in the smallest way, love becomes how we overcome our challenges *together*. That's just the way God planned it. We need one another. One important thing we can do is pray for those who are facing a hard time. God's comfort can be felt through the prayers of others.

BIG QUESTIONS

1. How do you show compassion to someone who is hurting?

2. God chooses us to express His compassion in the world. What do you have a "soft heart" for—homeless people, the hungry, animals, the environment? List three areas where you'd like to be a blessing.

3. Can you think of some ways to put compassion into action in your school or community?

WORDS AND WISDOM TO SHARE

As a family, choose one thing in your community or the world that you feel compassionate about. Together, decide how you can help lighten the burden of those affected—and pray for them each day this week.

GOD AND ME

God is always gentle, compassionate, and kind. Write down some things that have stirred your compassion this week—toward a friend, a family member, a teacher, or people you might not even know who are dealing with a hard situation. Take time to pray for them.

WEEK #29

Treat Everyone the Same

DAILY READINGS & REFLECTIONS

Day 1: Meet Joel (from Joel 1).
Joel was a prophet who warned the Israelites about God's coming punishment for their sins. He urged them to be truly sorry, and to make a real and lasting change.

Day 2: Read Joel 2:21–27.
God forgives our wrongdoing and gives us a chance to start over. Like Him, we should offer another chance to those who disappoint us. A new start is a gift.

Day 3: "The Lord will be a refuge for His people, a stronghold for the people of Israel." (from Joel 3:16)
God is a refuge—we can talk to Him in prayer anytime.

Day 4: "They trample on the heads of the poor as on the dust of the ground and deny justice to the oppressed." (from Amos 2:7)
God's people were being unkind to the poor—once again turning away from God and His commandments. A godly response is always humble, caring, and kind.

Day 5: Read Amos 4:13.
Amos reminded the Israelites that God forms the mountains and creates the wind. God wants us to observe what He created, so we're aware of His presence around us.

Day 6: "Seek good, not evil, that you may live. Then the Lord God Almighty will be with you, just as you say He is." (from Amos 5:14)
Be kind. Everyone is valued and loved by God.

Day 7: Meet Amos (from Amos 7:10–15).
Amos was a shepherd and farmer. Some people thought he wasn't qualified to be a prophet who spoke God's words. But God uses people of small **stature** to do great things.

The books of Joel and Amos show that God, as a loving Father, disciplines His people when they go against Him. The Israelites were following the ways of a king who did everything God was against. They were being unfair to the poor. They were treating the innocent, needy, and helpless in unkind ways. It was breaking God's heart. But these books also tell us that God's love and forgiveness turns everything around in time.

God cares deeply for those who are treated unfairly. His heart is filled with sympathy for people who are alone, in need, or feel unloved. When we follow God and learn to love Him with all our heart, we get better and better at loving others.

BIG QUESTIONS

1. When you treat a friend or family member in the wrong way, how do you correct it?

2. How do you feel when you're kind? How do you feel when you're unkind?

GOD AND ME

There will always be people who are suffering. Take time to write a prayer you can bring to God for those who are hurting.

WEEK #30

Follow God with a Happy Heart

DAILY READINGS & REFLECTIONS

Day 1: "The pride of your heart has deceived you." (from Obadiah 1:3)
A proud heart will **deceive** you. A heart that loves God believes in kindness, forgiveness, generosity, and helping others.

Day 2: Meet Jonah (from Jonah 1).
Jonah was a Hebrew prophet who was given specific instructions from God, but he didn't listen. When we disobey God, He uses our choices to teach us.

Day 3: Read Jonah 2.
Even when we make mistakes, God loves us. As soon as you realize you've gone the wrong way, God is there to love you, forgive you, and guide you back to Him.

Day 4: Read Jonah 3.
When Jonah obeyed God, an entire city turned away from their sinful ways. God can do great things through us when we choose to do the right things through Him!

Day 5: Meet Micah (from Micah 1:1–2).
Micah was a prophet from a small town where the powerful and wealthy would **oppress** the poor. He warned God's people of the consequences of their actions.

Day 6: Read Micah 5:2–4.
God gave us hope through the prophets in the Old Testament. In these verses, Micah shares God's promise of our Savior and King, Jesus Christ.

Day 7: "And what does the Lord require of you? To act justly and to love mercy and to walk humbly with your God." (from Micah 6:8)
When you do what is good and humble in God's eyes, He blesses you.

The books of Obadiah, Jonah, and Micah show us how important it is to obey God. These prophets warned God's people of the judgment coming as a result of their disobedient ways. The people were proud and looked down on the less fortunate. They didn't protect the innocent, or offer fairness to the poor. God's heart is always tender toward those who are poor and suffering—and ours should be the same.

When we feel sad or a little down in the dumps, it's a good time to think about what we've spent our time doing. It's hard to feel unhappy when we're doing things to please God and help people. Everything we do has a ripple effect, like throwing a stone into a pond. Things like taking the time to study with a friend because they want to do well on a test, choosing to hang out with a classmate who needs a friend, or being the one to stop a conversation with friends that would hurt someone's feelings are all things that cause a ripple effect of goodness.

BIG QUESTIONS

1. Have you ever done something for someone else that made you feel happy? Write about that feeling here.

2. When you're making a decision, do you consider whether or not your actions reflect God's love before you follow through with them?

WORDS AND WISDOM TO SHARE

Make plans with your family to do three acts of goodness or charity. They can be small acts of love toward a neighbor, a surprise kindness for someone who serves you at a restaurant, or even an extra walk for your pet. Talk about the joy your actions bring to you and to others!

WEEK #31

Remember God Is Good

DAILY READINGS & REFLECTIONS

Day 1: "The Lord is good, a refuge in times of trouble. He cares for those who trust in Him." (from Nahum 1:7)
Following God is the best way to make the world better.

Day 2: Meet Habakkuk (from Habakkuk 1:1–4).
Habakkuk was a prophet who found it hard to trust God when so much darkness was in the world. God is good even when bad things happen.

Day 3: "Lord, I have heard of Your fame; I stand in awe of Your deeds, Lord." (from Habakkuk 3:2)
When Habakkuk remembered God's miracles, it helped him trust that God is always working in the hearts of people.

Day 4: "Seek the Lord, all you humble of the land, you who do what He commands. Seek righteousness, seek humility." (from Zephaniah 2:3)
Seeking God leads to good things.

Day 5: Read Zephaniah 3:17.
God sings in celebration of you! His heart is bursting with joy for you.

Day 6: Meet Haggai (from Haggai 1:13).
God had done a good thing for His people by returning them to their homeland. Haggai reminded them to put God first and to serve Him faithfully.

Day 7: Read Haggai 2:4–5.
Be strong, work hard, and don't be afraid! Every good thing we have and every brave thing we do is because God is with us.

In the books of Nahum, Habakkuk, Zephaniah, and Haggai, people's bad behavior reflects how far they had strayed from the goodness of God. Sometimes we have questions about God's goodness when we see the wrongs and suffering in our world. We can't know how God's promise and plan will unfold. But it's up to us to remember to look for the good things God is doing, and jump in to be a part of them. Doing good shows our trust in God's good plan.

If we ever wonder about God's faithfulness, we need only to watch the sun rise every morning. If we wonder about trusting God when we're hurting, we need only to think about the people in our lives who hug us and say, "I love you." If we wonder how much God cares, we simply need to stand on a beach and remember that His thoughts of us outnumber the grains of sand.

BIG QUESTIONS

1. What are your favorite *good things* in your life and in God's big world?

____

____

____

2. When you're struggling to remember how good God is, what do you do?

____

____

____

GOD AND ME

Take some quiet time to finish these sentences:

God is good because ______________________________.

I see God's goodness when I look at ______________________________.

I remember how good God is every time ______________________________.

I feel like I'm part of God's goodness in the world when I ______________________________.

WEEK #32

God Keeps His Promises

DAILY READINGS & REFLECTIONS

Day 1: Meet Zechariah (from Zechariah 1:1–3).
God sent the prophet Zechariah to the Israelites when they returned to the land God promised them.

Day 2: Read Zechariah 7:8–10.
We are created in God's image to be like Him here on earth. Sympathy for those who are suffering, generosity for those in need, and fair treatment of all people are gifts of God's love.

Day 3: "Do not be afraid. These are the things you are to do: Speak the truth to each other, and render true and sound judgment in your courts." (from Zechariah 8:15–16)
Telling the truth is *always* the right thing to do.

Day 4: "See, your king comes to you, righteous and victorious, lowly and riding on a donkey." (from Zechariah 9:9)
This verse tells how the Savior would enter the city of Jerusalem during His time on earth.

Day 5: "Do we not all have one Father? Did not one God create us?" (from Malachi 2:10)
We are all equal in worth and equally *worthy* of God's love.

Day 6: Read Malachi 3:6–12.
Not only will heaven's blessings fill you up, they'll overflow into every part of your life.

Day 7: "Those who feared the Lord talked with each other, and the Lord listened and heard." (from Malachi 3:16)
Fear of the Lord means we respect and honor God.

The books of Zechariah and Malachi encourage God's people to return to Him. The prophets knew that God's promise to restore the world was going to come true. Even though God's people had suffered while turning away from Him, His love always held them close. God is full of compassion. He always makes a way to mend our relationship with Him. God tells us that following Him means loving one another, speaking the truth, and treating one another equally.

God tells us something else through the prophets of the Old Testament: A Savior would be born into our world, to sacrifice His life for the forgiveness of our sins. When God fulfilled this promise, our relationship with Him was mended forever! God gives good promises to us and He keeps them all. When you promise your parents that you'll clean your room, help with the dishes, or do better in school, do you ever let them down? It's something we all do. But God's love for us is dependable and sure. He will never break a promise He makes.

BIG QUESTIONS

1. When you make a promise to someone, do you ask God to help you keep it? How?

2. After you've broken a promise to someone, how do you correct this? Ask God for advice if you're unsure.

WORDS AND WISDOM TO SHARE

Gather some of your closest friends to talk about ways you can follow God more closely. How can you help one another commit to this?

WEEK #33
Oh, the Miracle of You!

DAILY READINGS & REFLECTIONS

Day 1: Meet Joseph (from Matthew 1:18–25).
Joseph was the earthly father of Jesus, the Messiah. Joseph was an important part of Jesus's life—which was marked by miracles from beginning to end!

Day 2: Meet John the Baptist (from Matthew 3).
John the Baptist is an inspiring example of someone who lived His purpose with passion. He prepared the way for the coming of Jesus.

Day 3: Read Matthew 5:1–16.
You are an amazing miracle of God. What others say about you isn't true if it doesn't align with what God says about you.

Day 4: "Are not two sparrows sold for a penny? Yet not one of them will fall to the ground outside your Father's care." (from Matthew 10:29–30)
God is paying attention to you, every minute of every day.

Day 5: Read Matthew 14:22–32.
Jesus walked on water to be with His disciples. He would do anything to be near to us, too!

Day 6: "Jesus said, 'Let the little children come to me, and do not hinder them, for the kingdom of heaven belongs to such as these.'" (from Matthew 19:14)
Children hold the key to heaven. You have more to teach the world than you realize.

Day 7: "Jesus replied: 'Love the Lord your God with all your heart and with all your soul and with all your mind [and love] your neighbor as yourself.'" (from Matthew 22:37–39)
Love, love, love. God's most important commandment.

The book of Matthew records many miracles Jesus did when He lived on earth. When you read through them, you see that nothing is impossible for God. And He created *you*.

There is no one else like you. You are a one-time miracle of divine design. This is what you have to remember when others see you differently than God does. It helps to consider that maybe they've forgotten *they're* a miracle, too! It's hard to treat others with kindness when we forget how much God loves us.

If you have a sibling, you can understand more clearly how we're all created differently. Things you do might get on their nerves, and vice versa. Maybe you're neat and they're messy, or you're messy and they're neat! There might be challenges to keeping your cool with your siblings or friends because of differences and habits. Seeing them the way God does—divinely designed miracles worthy of love—can help us be patient. When we learn to see everyone through the lens of God's love, it softens our heart.

BIG QUESTIONS

1. What miracle from the Bible has made an impact on you?

2. How does it make you feel to know you're one of God's miracles?

3. What are some traits you've learned about Jesus that you want to bring into your life?

WORDS AND WISDOM TO SHARE

Get together with your family or friends. Bring snacks! Put your names in a hat and have everyone draw from it. Write down what is different from you and the person you've drawn. Write down what you like best about them. Finally, write down a miracle you'd like to see God do for them.

GOD AND ME

You are a miracle from head to toe. God knew you before you were born. Think of the things that make you unique and write a prayer to thank Him for making you, *you*.

WEEK #34

Don't Be Afraid!

DAILY READINGS & REFLECTIONS

Day 1: **"Very early in the morning, while it was still dark, Jesus got up, left the house and went off to a solitary place, where He prayed." (from Mark 1:35)**
Spending time alone in prayer is a special way to be close to God.

Day 2: **Meet the 12 Disciples of Jesus (from Mark 3:13–19).**
Jesus chose twelve men to follow Him during His earthly ministry. We can ask God to bring friends into our life who can teach us and encourage us.

Day 3: **"He got up, rebuked the wind and said to the waves, 'Quiet! Be still!' Then the wind died down and it was completely calm. He said to His disciples, 'Why are you so afraid? Do you still have no faith?'" (from Mark 4:39–40)**
Trust God for the courage to conquer *any* fear.

Day 4: **Meet Jairus (from Mark 5:21–43).**
Jairus had a daughter who was very sick. He pleaded with Jesus to make her well. When it seemed that all hope was gone, Jesus said, "Don't be afraid; just believe" (Mark 5:36).

Day 5: **Read Mark 9:2–8.**
Three disciples were given a glimpse of Jesus in His heavenly glory. It was a miracle that would strengthen their faith for what was to come.

Day 6: **"Sitting down, Jesus called the Twelve and said, 'Anyone who wants to be first must be the very last, and the servant of all.'" (from Mark 9:35)**
Putting others first and serving others are qualities of being a good leader.

Day 7: **"Jesus said, '. . . this poor widow has put more into the treasury than all the others. They all gave out of their wealth; but she, out of her poverty, put in everything.'" (Mark 12:43–44)**
Giving something up for the sake of others is the kind of giving God values most.

The book of Mark is the second of four books that cover the life of Jesus. It holds many teachings that remind us to be brave. Did you know God tells us not to be afraid hundreds of times in the Bible? We are capable of doing courageous things when we trust Him. Fear is the invisible force behind every doubt we face. One way to get past it is to learn about Jesus's life. He was *never* afraid. He trusted God completely and obeyed Him perfectly.

We're not perfect, but we can be inspired by Jesus's courage. We can look up to Him when things feel too big for us to handle. It can feel impossible to get through the sadness of losing a favorite pet. It can seem impossible to forgive the friend who has hurt our feelings again. It can feel impossible to stop the anger we feel when we're treated unfairly. Praying is the way through impossible things. God can help us manage our feelings and replace fear with faith. Jesus knew God could be trusted in every situation, and that trust made way for miracles.

BIG QUESTIONS

1. When do you feel afraid?

2. Can you think of a time when God gave you courage you didn't think you had?

3. What is your favorite Bible verse to pray when you need to conquer fear?

WORDS AND WISDOM TO SHARE

Interview a friend, family member, or church leader about their biggest fear. Ask them to describe the fear, and how they turn to God for help.

GOD AND ME

Draw a fear you'd like God's help with.

WEEK #35
The Way Love Gives

DAILY READINGS & REFLECTIONS

Day 1: Meet Zechariah (from Luke 1:5–25).
Zechariah was a Jewish priest, and the father of John the Baptist. He was visited by an angel of the Lord, who brought good news to him and his wife.

Day 2: Meet the Virgin Mary (from Luke 1:26–56).
Mary is the woman God chose to be Jesus's mother. Our heavenly Father's plan for Mary's life was greater than she could have imagined.

Day 3: Read Luke 2:1–21.
An angel announced Jesus's birth to shepherds in the fields. They were told He would be in a manger. From birth, the message Jesus brought is one of humility and sacrifice.

Day 4: "John answered, 'Anyone who has two shirts should share one with the one who has none, and anyone who has food should do the same.'" (from Luke 3:11)
God asks us to share with others when they're in need. Love gives in many ways.

Day 5: Read Luke 10:25–37.
Love God and love our neighbor. These are the most important commandments.

Day 6: Read Luke 15:11–32.
The **prodigal** son lost his way, but returned to the open arms of the father who loved him. We might stray from the shelter of God's love, but He will always celebrate our return.

Day 7: "Zacchaeus...said to the Lord, '...Here and now I give half of my possessions to the poor, and if I have cheated anybody out of anything, I will pay back four times the amount.'" (from Luke 19:8)
Zacchaeus learned the power of God's love when he met Jesus.

The book of Luke gives more details of Jesus's life. There's no greater example of God's love, or the way love gives, than Jesus. Love gives willingly. Love gives generously. Love gives so those in need are fed, so the elderly feel respected and honored, so the poor know they're cared for, so neighbors know they aren't alone. Love gives in every way possible, so our lives are brighter reflections of God.

Love isn't always an easy thing to give. When there are people who don't act in a kind and loving way toward us, it's hard to respond kindly to them. But Jesus tells us to love those who are unkind. He asks us to pray for them. We can play a small part in showing them how much God loves them.

There are people and things that are easy to love—our family, friends, pets, and home. But we'll be challenged over and over again to share God's love when we don't think others deserve it. Those are the tests God loves to see us pass.

BIG QUESTIONS

1. Have you ever been challenged to respond with kindness when it was hard to do?

2. What is your favorite way to share God's love?

3. What are some ways you and your family have helped those in need?

WORDS AND WISDOM TO SHARE

As a family, discuss a few ways you want to reflect to your community how *love gives*. You might look up local charities, causes you'd like to support, or nursing homes you can visit. See if you can build a group to meet every season and volunteer in your community.

GOD AND ME

Ask God to show you some ways to express love to someone who really needs it. Write down what you feel in your heart, and then how it feels to follow through!

WEEK #36

The Power of Love & Friendship

DAILY READINGS & REFLECTIONS

Day 1: Meet Nicodemus (from John 3:1–8).

Nicodemus was a **Pharisee**, a religious leader who spoke to Jesus in secret. It's okay to have questions for God. The Bible reveals answers.

Day 2: Read John 4:43–54.

Jesus knew that many people would have to "see to believe." He offered signs and performed miracles to reveal God's love.

Day 3: "Here is a boy with five small barley loaves and two small fish, but how far will they go among so many?" (from John 6:9)

Jesus fed 5,000 people with one boy's lunch, one of the most amazing things He did.

Day 4: "The next day the great crowd that had come for the festival heard that Jesus was on His way to Jerusalem. They took palm branches and went out to meet Him." (from John 12:12–13)

This is the event we celebrate today as Palm Sunday, the week before Easter.

Day 5: Read John 15:9–17.

We are chosen by God to follow Him, and His command to us is, "Love each other."

Day 6: Read John 19.

When Jesus died on the cross, He did it in willing obedience to God. By giving His life, He made ours new again. This is the picture of God's love for us.

Day 7: "Now Mary stood outside the tomb crying. As she wept, she bent over to look into the tomb and saw two angels in white, seated where Jesus's body had been." (from John 20:11)

Hope is never gone, because God is always with us.

In the book of John, we see Jesus's life and God's love on full display. God's promise of a Savior came true in Jesus. God's love for us is forever true in the life Jesus gave for us. There's nothing in the universe that can make it fade or take it away.

We begin to understand the gifts of love and forgiveness when we're given another chance after we do something wrong. When the people we hurt accept our apology and don't bring up our mistakes again, God is shining through. Our heart feels relieved and we feel thankful.

Our friendship with God is the most valuable friendship in our lives, because it teaches us the way to love the *people* in our life. We can never forget that love matters most.

BIG QUESTIONS

1. How does it make you feel to know that Jesus gave His life because God loves you so much?

2. God chose you, and Jesus calls you His friend. In what ways does their love for you teach you how to love others?

3. God's love is more powerful than anything. What would you ask Him to help you with when it comes to being kind and forgiving others?

WORDS AND WISDOM TO SHARE

Get together as a family and choose an activity that conveys love and forgiveness, second chances, or the gift of friendship. You could pick a movie, or maybe you could even decide to read the book of John and have a family Bible study. Talk about what you learned and how you can carry the messages of love and forgiveness into all areas of your life.

GOD AND ME

Write down the qualities you think make Jesus a good friend. Do you share those qualities with Him? How do you share them with your friends?

WEEK #37

The Holy Spirit, Our Helper

DAILY READINGS & REFLECTIONS

Day 1: Read Acts 1:1–10.
It was hard for Jesus's disciples to see Him go back to heaven. But they soon became excited about the work He gave them to do.

Day 2: Meet the Holy Spirit (from Acts 2:36–47).
We have three divine beings in our life: God, Jesus, and the Holy Spirit. The Holy Spirit lives in us. He gives us the courage to live a big, purpose-filled life for God.

Day 3: Read Acts 3.
The disciples continued teaching about God's love, the way Jesus did. The resurrection opened the door to eternal life with God, and they wanted everyone to have that hope!

Day 4: Meet Saul (from Acts 9).
Saul turned to Jesus through a miraculous and personal encounter, and he became known as Paul the Apostle.

Day 5: Read Acts 15:6–11.
God accepts us just as we are. We don't need to earn God's love, Jesus's grace, or the Holy Spirit's gifts.

Day 6: "In everything I did, I showed you that by this kind of hard work we must help the weak, remembering the words the Lord Jesus himself said: 'It is more blessed to give than to receive.'" (from Acts 20:35)
We discover how true Jesus's words are when we help others.

Day 7: "For two whole years Paul stayed there…and welcomed all who came to see him. He proclaimed the kingdom of God and taught about the Lord Jesus Christ." (from Acts 28:30–31)
Paul was brave and unafraid when he taught others about Jesus.

The book of Acts is an exciting look at how the world continued to learn about Jesus. His death and resurrection became the disciples' megaphone for God's love and the hope of everlasting life. We also read about how the disciples received the gift that God promised and Jesus talked about: the Holy Spirit. Every part of the **Trinity** is on our side every moment of every day.

We can all feel alone at times. There might be days when our friends seem distant or uncaring. There might be times when it feels like your parents don't understand you completely, or you don't agree with their decisions. The Holy Spirit is a gift for good reason—God *never* wants you to feel alone. The Holy Spirit loves you with all His heart and listens to every word you say. There is nothing too small for Him to care about, or too big for Him to help you with.

BIG QUESTIONS

1. Do you ask the Holy Spirit to help you throughout your day?

2. What makes a gift from God priceless?

GOD AND ME

Draw a picture of the Holy Spirit as your personal superhero.

WEEK #38

Pray for Others

DAILY READINGS & REFLECTIONS

Day 1: "Since the creation of the world God's invisible qualities—His eternal power and divine nature—have been clearly seen, being understood from what has been made, so that people are without excuse." (from Romans 1:20)
God is in everything He created.

Day 2: Read Romans 5:1–5.
Suffering is a part of life. We can't compare our pain, but we can pray for each other.

Day 3: "And we know that in all things God works for the good of those who love Him, who have been called according to His purpose." (from Romans 8:28)
God wants us to trust Him and keep a good attitude.

Day 4: Read Romans 10:9–13.
Following God means believing in Jesus, and knowing He hears when we call on Him. Praying for others is a good reason to call on Him; His love will answer.

Day 5: Read Romans 12.
God asks us to bless those who are unkind and never try to get even. The loving response to unloving actions is to pray for those who do them.

Day 6: "Let no debt remain outstanding, except the continuing debt to love one another." (from Romans 13:8)
Loving God means we are filled with love to give others.

Day 7: Meet Phoebe (from Romans 16:1–2).
Phoebe was a deacon in the seaport church of Cenchreae. She helped Paul and many other people. Those who are willing to serve others make great leaders.

The Apostle Paul's letter to the Romans is filled with encouragement. Praying for others is one of the best ways we can show our love for God and for others. Love is the commandment that all the others rest on. Promising to pray for someone can become an easy thing to say, but we can forget to follow our words with action. Prayer is our privilege! We know God hears us, just as He heard King David, Solomon, and Esther.

The practice of praying in the morning and at night before we fall asleep is a good one. It can be a quiet time with our thoughts. We might remember hearing someone talk about a need they have, and we can pray for them. Maybe we'll think about someone we love but haven't seen for a while, and we can pray for them. There might be a sadness in our heart about something we heard or saw on television, and we can pray for help. Every prayer is an act of love, and every act of love brings us closer to God.

BIG QUESTIONS

1. Who have you prayed for today?

2. Can you think of a prayer God has answered for you?

3. Jesus taught the disciples how to pray. What would you want Jesus to teach you about prayer?

WORDS AND WISDOM TO SHARE

Ask everyone in your house if there's something you can take to God in prayer for them. Write out a simple prayer for each request and give it to them.

GOD AND ME

You talk to God when you pray and bring your worries or happiest moments to Him. This week, think about God's plan for you. Write down a prayer asking God what He wants for you.

WEEK #39

What Is Love?

DAILY READINGS & REFLECTIONS

Day 1: Read 1 Corinthians 1:26–31.
To think we are better than someone else is not a trait of love. God loves everyone equally.

Day 2: Meet Apollos (from 1 Corinthians 3:1–9).
Apollos was a teacher. He had a strong knowledge of scripture and understood that love is at the top of God's to-do list.

Day 3: Read 1 Corinthians 6:19–20.
God created us. Doing what is good for our health respects the work God has done, and reflects our love for Him and for ourselves.

Day 4: Read 1 Corinthians 11:23–26.
Jesus said, "Greater love has no one than this: to lay down one's life for one's friends" (John 15:13). **Communion** is the remembrance of the sacrifice Jesus made for us.

Day 5: Read 1 Corinthians 13:1–8.
No matter our accomplishments, if we are unkind, we've accomplished nothing. Love is the only thing we can give that will last forever, because it comes from God.

Day 6: "Do not be misled: 'Bad company corrupts good character.'" (from 1 Corinthians 15:33)
Who we choose to spend our time with influences everything we do. It's wise to pray for friends who know the importance of love, kindness, forgiveness, and truth.

Day 7: "Be on your guard; stand firm in the faith; be courageous; be strong. Do everything in love." (from 1 Corinthians 16:13–14)
When we do everything in love, everything is better.

The first book of Corinthians gives one of the best descriptions of love found in the Bible. Chapter 13 is a good one to memorize. It explains what love is and also what love *isn't*. Love doesn't encourage us to brag about finishing first or getting a better grade on a test. It isn't proud about having the coolest shoes or the nicest bicycle in the neighborhood. Love makes everyone feel valued. Love gives us the courage to say, "I'm sorry, please forgive me."

God asks us to put love first because it's the best way for His light to shine. His greatest expression of love for us is Jesus. The clearest way to love Him back is by obeying Him and loving every person in our life. It's not an accident when you become fast friends with the new kid at school. God has a reason for bringing you together. Maybe they can show you God's love in a way you haven't seen it before. Love is doing kind, thoughtful, selfless things in daily, meaningful, and simple ways.

BIG QUESTIONS

1. Can you think of at least three things you've done this week to spread kindness?

2. When we give love generously, it multiplies and comes back to us. In what ways have you felt God's love come back to you?

3. What are some small but thoughtful ways you show your parents and siblings you love them?

WORDS AND WISDOM TO SHARE

Plan a sleepover with your friends and start the night with a quick discussion of 1 Corinthians 13. Challenge one another to remember at least three characteristics of love from the book. Decide one thing each of you will do for your families this week to show how much you love them.

GOD AND ME

Think about the reasons you're thankful for God's love and write them here.

WEEK #40

Comfort Others

DAILY READINGS & REFLECTIONS

Day 1: Read 2 Corinthians 1:1–7.
God comforts us during the hard things we go through. When He does, we understand His love in a deeper way.

Day 2: "For no matter how many promises God has made, they are 'Yes' in Christ." (from 2 Corinthians 1:20)
We can trust God's promises because of Jesus.

Day 3: "The old has gone, the new is here! All this is from God, who reconciled us to himself through Christ." (from 2 Corinthians 5:17–18)
Sometimes it's hard to forget when we've done something wrong, but with Jesus we are given fresh starts.

Day 4: Read 2 Corinthians 7:1–4.
Following God can sometimes mean we walk away from friends who do not help us toward the good things God wants for us.

Day 5: Read 2 Corinthians 9:6–9.
When we offer comfort, forgiveness, and kindness to others, God's heart swells with joy.

Day 6: Read 2 Corinthians 10:1–5.
It can be really tough to keep our thoughts from running in the wrong direction. But remember, we have God on our side when we feel alone.

Day 7: "I will boast all the more gladly about my weaknesses, so that Christ's power may rest on me... For when I am weak, then I am strong." (from 2 Corinthians 12:9–10)
God comes to our rescue when we need Him, and never leaves us.

The second book of Corinthians begins with a good lesson: God carries us through hard times so we can comfort others through theirs. There will always be a need for a hug, an encouraging word, and a listening heart. Going through a loss that makes us sad or a challenge that makes us want to give up is a very familiar struggle for everyone. God knew we would need one another. That's why He never fails to be there for us.

Sometimes we go through trials at the same time. A natural disaster can affect a lot of people at once. God uses our mutual pain and suffering to help us carry one another through. Together we are stronger, and our strength comes from God. Then there are times when we go through struggles we don't share with anyone. But God knows our thoughts and our hearts, and He knows exactly how to lift us up.

Every comfort God gives to us will be used to help someone else through their difficulty. That's how His love works in and through us.

BIG QUESTIONS

1. What is something you're struggling with right now?

2. Who has God sent to help you through a sad time?

3. Has God shown you how to comfort someone else because you know just how they feel?

WORDS AND WISDOM TO SHARE

Create "comfort cards" with your friends and family. Choose an encouraging Bible verse, write a simple prayer, or make a list of uplifting phrases or words. Here are some examples:

I love your smile!

Keep being brave

Here's a hug

You are not alone

GOD AND ME

Write a prayer for someone who is going through a hard time.

WEEK #41

The Good Fruit of God

DAILY READINGS & REFLECTIONS

Day 1: "Am I now trying to win the approval of human beings, or of God?… If I were still trying to please people, I would not be a servant of Christ." (from Galatians 1:10)
Following God and doing what's right matters more than anyone else's approval.

Day 2: "God does not show favoritism." (from Galatians 2:6)
Everyone is valued in God's eyes, and He loves us unconditionally.

Day 3: "The only thing that counts is faith expressing itself through love." (from Galatians 5:6)
We show how we love God by the way we love others.

Day 4: Read Galatians 5:13–18.
It's not surprising to God that we do things we know we shouldn't do. Following God isn't always easy, but it is always best.

Day 5: Read Galatians 5:22–26.
The Spirit of God produces good fruit in our life. His love grows in us and makes good things happen from the inside out.

Day 6: "Carry each other's burdens, and in this way you will fulfill the law of Christ." (from Galatians 6:2)
Helping others carry their sadness, fear, or rejection is like walking up to a person waiting at the door and opening it for them.

Day 7: Read Galatians 6:7–10.
We should take every chance we get to put a spotlight on God's love by doing good things for others. Kindness is a fruit produced by the Spirit of God living inside us.

The book of Galatians teaches us about the fruit of the Holy Spirit. It grows in us when we follow God. Its purpose is sharing God's love with the world. We're not created to hide what God gives us. You have special qualities that allow God to produce something different in you, something unlike anyone else. You might be naturally good at talking in front of a group, explaining the rules of a game, or making people laugh. You might be good at encouraging others to keep trying, listening to them when they're sad, or taking the time to make them feel important.

Whatever gifts you have, God wants you to use it! Not only is it good for others, it's good for us, too. When we're able to help someone understand their worth to a loving God, it grows our faith in how much God values us. Some things are beyond measure, and God's love for us is one of them.

BIG QUESTIONS

1. How do you think your "spiritual fruit" helps others?

2. What do people see in you that you're thankful God has given to you?

GOD AND ME

Draw a tree and fill it with the kind of fruit you'd like your life to produce. Write words on each fruit that describe your unique qualities and strengths.

WEEK #42

You Are Chosen by God

DAILY READINGS & REFLECTIONS

Day 1: Read Ephesians 1.
God chose you for His good purposes before He created the world! Everyone in your life knows they're blessed to have you—just the way God planned it to be.

Day 2: "For it is by grace you have been saved, through faith... For we are God's handiwork, created in Christ Jesus to do good works." (from Ephesians 2:8–10)
You are chosen, and you are a gift.

Day 3: Read Ephesians 3:14–21.
What God will do in our lives is more than you can imagine.

Day 4: Read Ephesians 4:29–32.
We are God's likeness in a watching world. We should speak kindly to those listening, forgive quickly those who offend us, and love fully those who feel unwanted.

Day 5: "Follow God's example, therefore, as dearly loved children and walk in the way of love." (from Ephesians 5:1–2)
Remind yourself every day that God picked you to walk in His way and love by His example.

Day 6: "Children, obey your parents in the Lord, for this is right. 'Honor your father and mother.'" (from Ephesians 6:1–2)
God chose your parents to love, guide, and care for you. You show Him love by honoring them.

Day 7: Read Ephesians 6:10–17.
We see many things in the world that are *not* like God. Our part is to become a bright light powered by God's love.

God chose you to follow Him before time began! The book of Ephesians holds messages about our special place in God's plan and how He prepares us to live a life of love. It's amazing to think God knew us before there were oceans, mountains, sun, or sky. Our world is a miraculous and beautiful expression of our good and glorious God. He designed the earth with love. Before the earth came to be, He chose you for good and meaningful purposes.

Our world is very different now than it was when the Apostle Paul was here. But the letters he wrote to those who believed in Jesus are still true. We can grow closer to God through every book in the Bible, and the stories and words in them can change our hearts. There are so many reasons to thank God for choosing us. By following Him, we learn the importance of honoring our parents. We understand the value of a humble heart. We find out that God desires a friendship with us, and there's no truer friendship than His.

BIG QUESTIONS

1. How do you show that you're thankful for God's choices in your life?

2. What is the best choice God made for you?

3. How do you see God working to build your faith and draw you closer to Him?

WORDS AND WISDOM TO SHARE

Choosing to put love into action is something we have to do on purpose. Get together with your friends and write thank-you notes to three people in your life.

GOD AND ME

Write down three different prayers you can pray for others using Paul's prayers for the Ephesians as a starting point. You'll find his prayers in chapters 1 and 3.

WEEK #43
Being Unselfish

DAILY READINGS & REFLECTIONS

Day 1: Read Philippians 2:1–11.
When God says, "value others above yourselves" and "put the needs of others first," He knows we can't do it alone. It takes practice. We need His help.

Day 2: "Do everything without grumbling or arguing, so that you may become blameless and pure." (from Philippians 2:14–15)
Being unselfish and thankful makes us glow like stars in the night sky.

Day 3: Meet Epaphroditus (from Philippians 2:25–30).
The description Paul gave of his friend Epaphroditus is heartwarming. When we trust and follow God, He gives us good friends and teaches us to care for others.

Day 4: "Forgetting what is behind and straining toward what is ahead, I press on toward the goal." (from Philippians 3:13–14)
The prize for following God is eternal life in heaven with Jesus.

Day 5: Read Philippians 4:4–9.
Where our thoughts go, our actions follow. When we think about what is true, pure, good, noble, and right, it helps us control our emotions.

Day 6: "I know what it is to be in need, and I know what it is to have plenty. I have learned the secret of being content in any and every situation. I can do all this through him who gives me strength." (from Philippians 4:12–13)
Being thankful makes it easier to be content.

Day 7: "My God will meet all your needs according to the riches of His glory in Christ Jesus." (from Philippians 4:19)
God gives peace. God gives courage. God promises to meet us where we are.

The book of Philippians gives us wisdom for living a life that honors God. You've probably discovered that standing in faith isn't always easy. Believing God is always with us is a challenge. We're reminded in this book that we can do all things through Christ, who gives us strength! We can be kind and unselfish, even when it's the last thing we feel like doing. You won't always feel like being kind to your sibling when they borrow something without asking or insist on choosing what to watch on television. These small challenges can teach you bigger lessons.

God uses everything to build our character and strengthen us. Being like God means being whole and knowing we don't need anything else to live a life filled with love and purpose. When we focus on loving others over getting our way, being selfless and kind comes easier. God is love by every definition. Love is unselfish, and God wants us to be that way, too.

BIG QUESTIONS

1. Can you remember acting in a selfish way this week? How did it make you feel afterward?

2. Do you have more trouble being kind at home or at school? Why do you think that is?

3. What is one way you can practice being kind every day?

WORDS AND WISDOM TO SHARE

Talk to your parents about starting a kindness jar. Whenever someone in your family does an act of kindness, at home or away from home, remember it and write it on a piece of paper to put in the jar. At the end of the week, sit together and read them.

GOD AND ME

Paul reminds us that we can do *all* things through Christ, who strengthens us. List the qualities of love that are most challenging for you. Focus your prayers on them and ask God to make you stronger.

WEEK #44

Guarding Our Words

DAILY READINGS & REFLECTIONS

Day 1: Meet Epaphras (from Colossians 1:3–8).
Epaphras was a preacher and a prayer warrior. Prayer is a power nothing on earth can stop and nothing in heaven can ignore.

Day 2: "We continually ask God to fill you with...understanding that the Spirit gives, so that you may live a life worthy of the Lord." (from Colossians 1:9–10)
The Holy Spirit helps us understand how to live a life that pleases God.

Day 3: Read Colossians 1:15–20.
Jesus was the image of the invisible God. In Him, all things were created. You are one of God's favorite creations. Jesus made the way for your spiritual rebirth.

Day 4: "Just as you received Christ Jesus as Lord, continue to live your lives in Him...strengthened in the faith as you were taught, and overflowing with thankfulness." (from Colossians 2:6–7)
Being thankful is the key to loving others.

Day 5: "Set your hearts on things above, where Christ is, seated at the right hand of God. Set your minds on things above, not on earthly things." (from Colossians 3:1–2)
God teaches us that what we think about most, we care about most.

Day 6: Read Colossians 3:12–14.
It's all about love—our purpose, God's plan, and everything in between!

Day 7: "Let your conversation be always full of grace, seasoned with salt, so that you may know how to answer everyone." (from Colossians 4:6)
God gives us wisdom freely and abundantly when we ask for it.

The book of Colossians holds lessons for keeping our mind on heaven, speaking good words, and covering ourselves in kindness and patience. Paul mentions his friend, Epaphras, who was dedicated to praying for others. Over and over again, we learn the importance of having good friends. Following God sets us apart from the world, and having friends who encourage us is essential to our growing relationship with God.

God created the world with words, and words are powerful. God wants our conversations to be filled with kindness. He wants us to guard what we say, because words can stay in our mind long after we hear them. Negative words tend to stick around the longest. When someone lies about us or teases us, it can make us feel insecure. We might question our worth, or whether or not others will like us.

When bad thoughts try to make us forget what God says about us, that's when we have to remember what we've learned. God pays such close attention that He collects your tears, and nothing in the universe can keep Him from loving you. You're a *big* deal in the eyes of a *big* God—and that's what matters most.

BIG QUESTIONS

1. When do you find it most difficult to control what you say?

2. Can you think of someone other than God who encourages you?

GOD AND ME

Draw a picture inspired by the phrase **GUARD YOUR WORDS**. Ask God to give you the strength to stop speaking negative words and start speaking what is good and pleasing to Him.

WEEK #45

Rejoice Always, Pray Continually

DAILY READINGS & REFLECTIONS

Day 1: Read 1 Thessalonians 1.
An important part of living for God is praying for others.

Day 2: "When you received the word of God...you accepted it not as a human word, but as it actually is...at work in you who believe." (from 1 Thessalonians 2:13)
The word of God is actively working within us.

Day 3: Read 1 Thessalonians 3:12–13.
These verses are a prayer from the Apostle Paul for believers.

Day 4: Read 1 Thessalonians 5:12–24.
When someone pops into your head, say a quiet prayer for them. When you're about to take a test, say a quiet prayer for wisdom and peace. Praying is easy when we form the habit.

Day 5: "Your faith is growing more and more, and the love all of you have for one another is increasing." (from 2 Thessalonians 1:3)
When God gave us the gift of Jesus, His love for us was revealed.

Day 6: Read 2 Thessalonians 3:6–10.
Work is a blessing from God. Learning to work hard will help you understand its importance. Discipline and hard work come with rewards.

Day 7: "Never tire of doing what is good." (from 2 Thessalonians 3:13)
When you trust God to make you strong, you never get tired of doing good.

The first and second books of Thessalonians focus on Jesus's return, staying strong in our faith, working hard, and praying continually. We've learned about the importance of praying for others, and it's a message worth repeating. In this book, Paul tells the believers to pray continually. The silent prayers we say throughout our day make us feel less anxious and closer to God.

You face many things that stir up emotions, all day long. In the same day, you can go from feeling happy and excited to afraid and insecure. You might have a disagreement with a friend, or realize you forgot something at home while you're at school. You might get stressed by things that are out of your control, like the unkind actions of another person or a downpour that started while you were walking home.

This is when following the wisdom of God can turn everything around. Prayer can give us an immediate sense of calm and peace. We know God is listening. We have an unbeatable team that is always ready to help us: God, our heavenly Father; Jesus, our Savior and friend; and the Holy Spirit, our comforter and companion.

BIG QUESTIONS

1. What are some things that make you feel insecure or stressed?

2. Does it help you to pray when you feel anxious?

GOD AND ME

Make a list of scriptures about prayer. See if you can memorize one this week.

WEEK #46

Staying Faithful

DAILY READINGS & REFLECTIONS

Day 1: Meet Timothy (from 1 Timothy 1:1–7 and 2 Timothy 1:3–5).
The Apostle Paul called Timothy his "true son in the faith" (1 Timothy 1:2). Timothy was well-studied in the scriptures and raised by women of faith.

Day 2: Read 1 Timothy 2:1–6.
Pray for those in authority, that we may live peaceful and quiet lives in godliness and holiness. When we pray for leaders, we're blessing them and pleasing God.

Day 3: "Don't let anyone look down on you because you are young, but set an example." (from 1 Timothy 4:12)
God wants you to know you can be strong and faithful even when you're young.

Day 4: Read 1 Timothy 5:8.
God created families to be a reflection of His love and faithfulness. He planned for us to take care of one another and be examples of His unconditional love.

Day 5: "The Spirit God gave us does not make us timid, but gives us power, love and self-discipline." (from 2 Timothy 1:7)
God has given us the gift of the Holy Spirit to be our close and constant companion.

Day 6: Read 2 Timothy 2:22–26.
Pursue faith, love, and peace. Good things don't come from going along with the wrong things.

Day 7: "All Scripture is God-breathed and is useful for teaching." (from 2 Timothy 3:16)
Reading your Bible is the best way to prepare yourself to fulfill God's plan for your life.

The first and second books of Timothy are letters the Apostle Paul wrote to his young apprentice. They are written to encourage sound teaching of the way God wants us to live. We're given instructions to pray for our leaders, take care of our families, and run from the things that are unlike God. Staying faithful to God is a decision and a discipline. God has given us everything we need to be successful!

Loving God and loving people is the clear and simple way to follow the wisdom of the Bible. Jesus tells us that every other commandment we're given hangs on the first two: love God and love your neighbor. Have you ever had a hard time understanding the instructions your teacher gives you? Jesus makes obeying God clear by teaching us to love. Love tells us to be kind, even to those who aren't kind to us. Love tells us to share with our friends and siblings, even when we don't feel like it. Love tells us to hope when things look impossible, to trust God when we're afraid, and to believe everything is working together for our good.

BIG QUESTIONS

1. What do you think was the most helpful instruction in the books of Timothy?

2. What are some of your favorite things about the family God has given you?

GOD AND ME

Being faithful to God means trusting Him no matter what happens. Write down some things you've gone through that have tested your faith. How did they challenge you to trust God? Can you look back and see how God helped you become stronger?

WEEK #47

Be Gentle Toward Everyone

DAILY READINGS & REFLECTIONS

Day 1: **Meet Titus (from Titus 1).**
Paul addresses Titus as "my true son in our common faith" (Titus 1:4). Following God is the best way to live, and it's important to have friends and mentors to help us.

Day 2: **"In everything set them an example by doing what is good." (from Titus 2:7)**
In everything we say and do, God should be lifted up.

Day 3: **Read Titus 2:11–14.**
God tells us to say no to whatever distracts us from our commitment to Him.

Day 4: **"Remind the people to be subject to rulers and authorities, to be obedient, to be ready to do whatever is good." (from Titus 3:1)**
God knows being obedient to those in authority strengthens our willingness to be obedient to Him.

Day 5: **"Be peaceable and considerate, and [always be] gentle toward everyone." (from Titus 3:2)**
It can be a challenge to be gentle and considerate with siblings, friends, parents, and even people we don't know well. But with God's help, it can be done.

Day 6: **Read Titus 3:3–8.**
Paul tells us we should devote our life to doing what is good. God has shown us the perfection of love and goodness through the gift of Jesus.

Day 7: **Meet Philemon (from Philemon 1).**
This book is a letter Paul wrote to his friend Philemon concerning **Onesimus**. When someone believes in Jesus and accepts His sacrifice, God forgives them, and so should we.

The books of Titus and Philemon bring us more teaching from Paul the Apostle. We know love is the best way to share God's way in the world. When we serve God with a willing heart, we understand that both wisdom and love are gentle. To be gentle means to be patient. Patience is a quality of love that tests us the most. There are many little things that push us past our patience and into frustration or anger. If we ask God to help us, we can turn every single one of them into an opportunity to grow.

By learning to be patient, we'll get better at being gentle. Gentleness is kind and calm. It helps us keep a good attitude. When your parents give you an answer you don't like, or a sibling picks on you, patience will lead you to a calm response. As with anything we want to be good at, patience takes practice. That's why we should be determined to turn everything that tests our patience into a chance to reflect God's love.

BIG QUESTIONS

1. What little things test your patience the most every day? How do you ask God for help?

2. How can you work to be gentle even when you're angry?

GOD AND ME

Draw some things that make you most impatient, frustrated, or angry. Think about how you can ask God to help you be more calm and patient with them.

WEEK #48

Be Confident in God

DAILY READINGS & REFLECTIONS

Day 1: Read Hebrews 1:1–3.
Jesus is exactly like God, and He became human for us. He went through every emotion we feel, and trusted God's love to guide Him through.

Day 2: "Encourage one another daily." (from Hebrews 3:13)
What a wonderful habit to form.

Day 3: Read Hebrews 4:12–16.
The word of God is alive and active. We can be confident that when we read, understand, and memorize our Bible, it will change us in the most positive ways!

Day 4: "Because Jesus lives forever, He has a permanent priesthood. Therefore He is able to save completely those who come to God through Him, because He always lives to intercede for them." (from Hebrews 7:24–25)
Jesus is praying for you. *Always.*

Day 5: "Now faith is confidence in what we hope for and assurance about what we do not see." (from Hebrews 11:1)
Have faith that good things will happen. God knows the plan for you.

Day 6: "Let us run with perseverance the race marked out for us, fixing our eyes on Jesus, the pioneer and perfecter of faith." (from Hebrews 12:1–2)
The way we live a life of love and kindness is by focusing on Jesus.

Day 7: Read Hebrews 12:4–14.
God allows us to go through things that strengthen our faith.

The book of Hebrews is a confidence builder. We learn that Jesus is praying for us. We're reminded that He understands our feelings because He experienced every human emotion while He lived on earth. We are told we're running a race, and we can look forward to winning with confidence. There are many things that can shake our confidence in what we believe. God never turns away from our questions. Instead, He shows us how involved He is in our life.

On your down days, God might show you He's paying close attention through something your friend says to you, or by working out something you've been worried about. It might be something small that only God knows about, like finding that item you thought you'd lost, and it makes you happy. Each time God shows you He's with you, in a big or small way, you become more confident in your faith. That's what makes God happy.

BIG QUESTIONS

1. What are you most confident about in your life right now?

2. How does reading your Bible make you more confident in God's love for you?

3. Who has God put in your life to encourage you and make you feel brave?

WORDS AND WISDOM TO SHARE

Showing God's love to others is a good way to build our confidence in God's love for us. When we give love, it comes back to us in greater measure! Choose a neighbor to bless this week. Talk with your parents about things you might do for them.

GOD AND ME

In the space below, write down the things you feel confident about and the things you feel unsure about. Look for verses in the Bible about hope and courage.

I feel confident about . . . ______

______

______

______

______

I feel unsure about . . . ______

______

______

______

______

WEEK #49

The Joy of a Test

DAILY READINGS & REFLECTIONS

Day 1: Read James 1:1–7.
When we struggle with things, we're not alone. Tough things happen to everyone. God tells us to be joyful when we're tested, because challenges help us grow.

Day 2: "Every good and perfect gift is from above, coming down from the Father of heavenly lights." (from James 1:17)
Every good thing comes from God.

Day 3: Read James 2:1–4.
Judging others by their outward appearance is something God tells us never to do. God sees the heart; we can't.

Day 4: "Who is wise and understanding among you? Let them show it by their good life, by deeds done in the humility that comes from wisdom." (from James 3:13)
Wisdom is a gift from God.

Day 5: "The wisdom that comes from heaven is first of all pure; then peace-loving, considerate, submissive, full of mercy and good fruit, impartial and sincere." (from James 3:17)
This is God's perfect definition of wisdom.

Day 6: Read James 4:6–12.
Have you ever resisted something, like forgiving a friend, sharing with your sibling, or listening to your parents? Those struggles come from a proud heart. To a humble heart, God pours out His favor.

Day 7: "The prayer of a righteous person is powerful and effective." (from James 5:16)
When we follow God with a pure heart, our prayers are powerful.

The book of James begins by instructing us to be joyful when we go through trials of different kinds. How can you be happy about having an argument with your best friend, being disciplined by your parents, or being suspended from a game? It seems like an impossible thing to ask. Why would we be joyful about things that are hard or hurtful to go through?

God knows we get stronger when we're challenged to follow Him and do the right thing. Being humble and forgiving is hard when you're treated unfairly. Being kind is hard when someone calls you a name. In the face of things that hurt our feelings or make us angry, we should *still* be kind. It's the right thing to do. It's what God wants us to *learn* to do.

The other thing we learn when we go through a tough situation is how to persevere. God wants us to learn that no matter how hard it gets to be kind and respectful, He gives us the courage to do it. When we learn how strong we can be, the next time we face a test, we'll handle it with confidence.

BIG QUESTIONS

1. What is something that tested your perseverance? How did you handle it?

2. How good are you at doing the right thing when you're tested?

GOD AND ME

When is it hardest for you to control your anger? Talk to God in prayer about the specific challenges you have.

WEEK #50
Have a Servant's Heart

DAILY READINGS & REFLECTIONS

Day 1: Read 1 Peter 1.
Peter puts an emphasis on being holy, because God is holy. Having a servant's heart and wanting to please God should lead to a holy life.

Day 2: "You are a chosen people...God's special possession." (from 1 Peter 2:9)
Acts of love shine a light on the people around us. Every time you serve others, you shed light in a dark world.

Day 3: Read 1 Peter 3:8–22.
A servant's heart is eager to do good! Ask your parents to help you plan a time to volunteer in your community once a month.

Day 4: "Each of you should use whatever gift you have received to serve others, as faithful stewards of God's grace." (from 1 Peter 4:10)
You can start right where you are to share your gifts with the world!

Day 5: Read 1 Peter 5:1–11.
We might want to repay someone who hurts us by hurting them. We should *never* do it. The truest weapon against bad behavior is good behavior.

Day 6: Read 2 Peter 1.
If we follow God, we serve Him without hesitation. Our actions should mimic God.

Day 7: "In keeping with His promise we are looking forward to a new heaven and a new earth, where righteousness dwells." (from 2 Peter 3:13)
God's promise is a world ruled by love and peace.

The first and second books of Peter teach us the value of living a holy life. God is holy, and we should be holy. When we seek God and His holiness, it does miraculous work in us. As we choose to be humble servants of God's kindness and love, our heart longs to be like Him. A servant's heart looks like many things: cleaning up our mess before we're asked to; picking up the litter in our community park; taking the dog for a walk; spending time with a friend who's feeling down; giving Mom a hug when she least expects it.

We sometimes think the little things we do don't mean that much to God. He not only sees each kind thing we do, He also sees what it does in the hearts of others. The people who get a glimpse of God's love through us are quietly praising *Him*. We can't know now how many lives are changed by our small acts of love and service, but one day we will find out. When God fulfills the promise of a new heaven and a new earth, like Peter talks about, we will know the full impact we've made.

BIG QUESTIONS

1. What gifts do you see God developing in you?

2. Can you think of some ways you've served others and shown God's love this week?

GOD AND ME

Ask God to show you how to use the special gifts you have to serve others. Write down a plan of action to get started!

WEEK #51

Love God with All Your Heart

DAILY READINGS & REFLECTIONS

Day 1: "God is light; in Him there is no darkness at all." (from 1 John 1:5)
Jesus tells us to let our light shine before others, so they see our good deeds and glorify God.

Day 2: Read 1 John 2:1–17.
John warns us: If we're hateful, the light of God is not in us. Kindness, forgiveness, and respect keep the light of God's love shining brightly in our life.

Day 3: "Dear children, let us not love with words or speech but with actions and in truth." (from 1 John 3:17–18)
God's love is shown through our actions.

Day 4: Read 1 John 4:7–21.
God is love. Whoever lives in love lives in God, and God in them.

Day 5: "This is the confidence we have in approaching God: that if we ask anything according to His will, He hears us." (from 1 John 5:14)
God's love motivates *every* decision He makes.

Day 6: Read 2 John 1.
John reminds us that loving our heavenly Father is the same as obeying Him.

Day 7: Read 3 John 1.
John tells us to imitate what is good. Acting like God is doing what is good. Following God leads to a life filled with every good thing He gives.

The books of John are a boost of encouragement to keep loving God with all our heart! We're also reminded to stay far away from the opposite of love: hate. Even the word sounds harsh to say. If we love God, our words should be filled with light. Think about what light does. The smallest light can be seen from miles away. The stars we see are trillions of miles from the earth. Light *travels*. Only God knows the effect of a single kind deed. It might be more far-reaching than we can imagine.

We can make a lasting difference, one kind deed at a time. You don't have to plan your entire future or search high and low for your purpose. God's purpose for us is to love one another. If we concentrate on that each day, we'll be doing our part to light up the whole world!

BIG QUESTIONS

1. Has God shown you, in some small way, the impact of a kind thing you've done?

2. In what ways do you see the light of God's love in your parents?

GOD AND ME

Write a prayer for each person in your family, and ask God to show you how to bless them and their good deeds.

WEEK #52
Our Forever Home

DAILY READINGS & REFLECTIONS

Day 1: Read Jude 1:17–25.
Jude warned us that there will be some who will abandon God to follow their own pursuits. To build up our faith, we can pray and read the Bible every day.

Day 2: Read Revelation 1:1–3.
The Apostle John was banished to the island of Patmos for preaching the salvation of Jesus Christ. While there, he was given a vision of the future of our world, and the world to come.

Day 3: "He placed His right hand on me and said: 'Do not be afraid. I am the First and the Last… I was dead, and now look, I am alive for ever and ever!'" (from Revelation 1:17–18)
When John saw Jesus again, he was overcome with fear and wonder.

Day 4: "The Lamb at the center of the throne will be their shepherd; 'he will lead them to springs of living water.' 'And God will wipe away every tear from their eyes.'" (from Revelation 7:17)
Our forever home is with God and Jesus.

Day 5: Read Revelation 15:3–4.
Singing and rejoicing is part of being happy and bursting with thankfulness. Heaven will be filled with song!

Day 6: Read Revelation 21:1–7.
Our home in heaven will be a place where there is no more death or crying or pain. God will make *everything* new.

Day 7: "Look, I am coming soon! My reward is with me, and I will give to each person according to what they have done." (from Revelation 22:12)
All things will happen according to God's perfect plan.

The book of Jude is one that is often overlooked, as it comes between John's third letter and the final book of the Bible, Revelation. But it's an important one, as Jude calls on us to be aware of false teachers. Coming from one of Jesus's brothers—Jude was one of Mary and Joseph's sons—it's an important reminder to keep our faith in God.

The book of Revelation lets us look ahead to the promise of spending eternity with Jesus as King. It's hard to imagine a world ruled by God's perfect love, but that's how it will be. Fear will be gone, pain will disappear, and crying will be no more. Jesus said, "Those who are victorious will inherit all this" (Revelation 21:7).

We have a lot to look forward to, but we have a lot to be thankful for right now, too. Thinking of reasons to be thankful every day helps us learn to be content. God planned for us to be here at this time in history, and every day holds a little bit of wonder if we pay attention. God loves when we share our love for Him with others, because it's filled with the hope the world needs. Every good thing God has wanted for us since the beginning of time is what we will have in our forever home—and being with Him is going to be the *best* part.

BIG QUESTIONS

1. What are you most thankful for about the home God has given you here?

2. Every act of kindness brings a little bit of God's love from heaven to earth. What have you done this week to share His love?

3. If you could design a house in our forever home, what would it look like and what would be in it?

WORDS AND WISDOM TO SHARE

Choose a movie to watch as a family. Pick one that has lots of laughter and a happy ending. Make sure everyone has their favorite snack and a cozy spot. Then simply enjoy the love around you in the room. Encourage everyone to share their thankfulness for one another.

GOD AND ME

Draw what you imagine heaven is like.

MY PRAYERS FOR MY FAITH-FILLED LIFE WITH GOD

Now that you've read about each book of the Bible and reflected on your growing relationship with God, write out your prayers for a life filled with abundance and faith. Remember that God is always with you—He knows your heart, and He loves you more than anything.

GLOSSARY

allegory: a story, poem, or picture that can be interpreted to reveal a hidden meaning

Communion: known as the Lord's Supper; a ritual done in remembrance of Jesus Christ's sacrifice for our sin

covenant: a sacred agreement between God and a person or group of people

cupbearer: an important official who guarded the king's cup from poisoning

deceive: to make someone believe something false is the truth

eternity: endless life after death

exalt: to raise high; to glorify or praise

holy: reflecting God's character; set apart from the world in pursuit of God

long-suffering: not quick to punish; being patient and restrained when angry

mercy: forgiveness that is an act of God's compassion and tender love

Messiah: a figure prophesied to be a savior or redeemer; anointed one

miracle: surprising event that can't be explained by natural or scientific laws; work of God

oppress: to give unfair or cruel treatment, usually by those in power

Pharisee: an important religious leader who was an expert in Jewish law

prodigal: a person who spends money in a reckless and wasteful way

repent: to turn from sin and restore our relationship with God

stature: importance based on qualities or abilities

temptation: the desire to do something wrong or unwise

Trinity: the Christian Godhead as one God in three persons: Father, Son, and Holy Spirit

PEOPLE & PRONUNCIATIONS

Absalom (**ab**-suh-l*uh*m) a beloved son of King David, who became proud and tried to steal the throne

Asaph (**asaf**) a Hebrew name meaning "gatherer"; Chief of the Levites appointed by King David to lead worship; a singer, prophet, and poet

Baruch (**baa**-rook) a Hebrew name meaning, "blessed"; a scribe (writer) and close friend of the prophet Jeremiah; he recorded Jeremiah's prophecies

Elihu (**eh**-li-hoo) a Hebrew name meaning, "my God is He"; the youngest and wisest of Job's friends; he counseled Job not to question God's ways

Eliphaz (**el**-uh-faz) a Hebrew name meaning, "God is pure gold"; one of the friends who visited Job at the time of his suffering

Epaphras (**eh**-pah-frahs) a passionate preacher of Jesus Christ and a fervent intercessor; a prayer warrior for the Colossians

Epaphroditus (eh-pah-froh-**di**-tus) a friend and fellow worker of the Apostle Paul; a member of the Philippian church who delivered aid to Paul when he was imprisoned in Rome

Ephraim (**ee**-free-uhm) a name used to refer to the *people of Israel* in the book of Hosea; they were the largest and most powerful tribe in northern Israel

Ezekiel (uh-**zee**-kee-uhl) a Hebrew name meaning "God will strengthen"; a prophet and priest who saw visions and prophesied for 22 years during the Israelite's exile in Babylon

Habakkuk (**haa**-buh-kuhk) a prophet who questioned God about the suffering and injustice he saw in the world

Haggai (**ha**-gai) Haggai was a prophet who instructed the Israelites to put God first and rebuild the temple; it would reflect their restored faithfulness to Him

Hanani (**hah**-nah-ni) a Hebrew name meaning "God is gracious"; brother of Nehemiah; because he was trustworthy and faithful, he was put in charge of the gates of Jerusalem

Hezekiah (hez-zuh-**kai**-uh) a Hebrew name meaning "God is my strength"; a righteous king of Judah, who followed God with all his heart

Hosea (ho-**zay**-uh) a Hebrew name meaning "salvation"; a prophet who married an unfaithful woman; Hosea's life was a metaphor for the Israelite's betrayal of their covenant with God and His faithfulness to forgive and restore them

Jehoshaphat (juh-**ho**-sha-fat) son of Asa, and the fourth king of Judah

Joab (joh-ab) King David's nephew; a military leader who also counseled King David

King Xerxes (king **zurk**-seez) a Persian ruler, known as Xerxes the Great; he chose Esther to be queen, which put her in the position to save the Jewish people

Mephibosheth (muh-**fi**-buh-sheth) the lame son of Jonathan; David faithfully cared for him as part of the covenant he made with Jonathan

Mordecai (**mor**-duh-kai) Esther's cousin, who took her in after she lost her parents; he was promoted by King Xerxes to second in command

Onesimus (uh-**neh**-suh-mus) a servant of Philemon who became a Christian through the teaching of Paul the Apostle; the subject of Paul's letter to Philemon

Othniel (**oth'**-ni-el) a Hebrew name meaning "God's lion"; the first judge of Israel, who delivered them from eight years of oppression

Philemon (fuh-**lee**-muhn) a friend and fellow worker of Paul the Apostle

Uzziah (u-**zai**-uh) a Hebrew name meaning, "the Lord is my strength"; a wealthy king who ruled Judah for 52 years

INDEX

G

H

I

J

K

L

M

N

O

P

R

S

T

U

W

Z

ACKNOWLEDGMENTS

The weight of this book felt overwhelming at times, but there were many people who helped with the heavy lifting.

Claire Herendeen has been a key part of my Callisto Publishing team from the beginning. She has the ability to send light and courage through an email. On more than one occasion, she guided me with hope when I felt smothered by fear and discouragement.

My editor, Pamela Bobowicz, is the everyday hero who carried this book to the finish line. Along the way there were obstacles I didn't think I could overcome. She picked me up throughout the journey and assured me God's grace was sufficient to carry us. Thank you, Pam—you're a gift.

I appreciate the talented editorial and design team at Callisto, who were the silent support system for the book. Without you, the book wouldn't be! I'm thankful for your hard work and commitment to excellence.

To Fred and Becky Merrill, who opened their home to me while I wrote the book. They prayed with me, encouraged me, cheered me on, and stood beside me in moments of helplessness with, "You can do this. God is faithful."

To my brothers, Steve, Rich, and Scott Rickner. Your love, compassion, and generosity have cleared pathways through the deepest valleys of my life. God has been so good to me through you, and I'm eternally grateful.

God has given me three daughters, but there is no way I could've imagined the blessing they would be. They have the incorruptible beauty of a gentle and quiet spirit, which is precious in God's sight and breathtaking in mine. Stephanie, Angela, and Ashley, you are pillars of love, friendship, and joy in my life every single day.

ABOUT THE AUTHOR

Bonnie Rickner Jensen loves writing for children of all ages. She spends most of her days in her slightly uncomfortable writing chair surrounded by stacks of books, trinkets from her travels, and fresh flowers. She's published more than 40 books for children and plans never to retire, feeling time and age will only make her rhymes and stories more interesting. There's always a stash of dark chocolate in her office she's almost willing to share, and a hug and a smile she's happily willing to give. Born in Ohio, she now calls sunny Florida home.